Commons and Borderlands

Commons and Borderlands

Working Papers on Interdisciplinarity,
Accountability and the
Flow of Knowledge

Marilyn Strathern

This edition first published in 2004 by

Sean Kingston Publishing

www.seankingston.co.uk

57 Orchard Way, Wantage, Oxon, OX12 8ED

©2004 Marilyn Strathern

British Library Cataloguing-in-Publication Data

A catalogue record for this book is available from the British Library

Printed by Lightning Source

ISBN 0–9545572–2–0

CONTENTS

PREFACE

Take various scientific disciplines, or disciplines from the humanities or from social science for that matter, and you will find interdisciplinary practice well entrenched. This does not deter current rhetoric, which sees new opportunities in new combinations of interests. One arresting strand is the promise that in a strong form – transdisciplinarity – 'society' might thereby be brought into 'science'. This collection of working papers addresses some of the background to early twenty-first-century interests in interdisciplinarity. The anthropologist's questions include the challenge that notions of property ownership pose to the expected flow of knowledge. A seminar series on 'Social Property' translates some of these challenges into debates, and this collection is designed to accompany that process. Equally well, the papers may be taken as independent pieces that reflect a particularly interesting era in the development of disciplines. They are left as open, unfinished, statements.

The Cambridge Social Property Seminar

Held in the University of Cambridge, and convened four times over 2004, the Social Property Seminar draws much of its colour from its immediate environment, and has its own particular focus. The issues which feed it, however, touch on very general dimensions of contemporary academic and scholarly life.

Basically, the topic – and the manner of its discussion – arises from recent moves within and beyond universities to value collaboration as a special source of creativity, to forge alliances between cognate disciplines, to experiment across the boundaries of academic disciplines and the performing arts, and to address diverse publics and non-academic interests. Desire for dialogue is not new: what is interesting about this moment in time is the institutional drive to embed such aspirations in new social forms. Three such enterprises in Cambridge provide the immediate stimulus: CRASSH (the Centre for Research in the Arts, Social Sciences and Humanities) is sponsor for a set of colloquia; the CGKP (Cambridge Genetics Knowledge Park) provides many of the substantive issues for debate; an interdisciplinary network called Crucible, which generates design and innovation processes, and offers professional design consultancy.

There are many appeals to the creative imagination in the promise to open up borders and cross into new territories. The Seminar asks, in that context, about certain ways or modes in which lines may be drawn, and the virtues or otherwise of doing so, and focuses on ownership as affording just such a mode. Ownership ranges from belonging, possession and exclusion, to rights of disposal exercised in transactions, primordial claims on the products of creativity, and property as the basis for profit. Four individual colloquia will address different practices of ownership across disciplines and across social contexts. Convened by James Leach (King's College Research Centre) and Alan Blackwell (Computer Laboratory), Interdisciplinary Design Workshops (IDWs) attached to each colloquium will treat debate as raw material for modelling/making processes and outputs.

The working papers provide some background to the colloquia topics. Working papers and colloquia in the seminar series are numbered in the same sequence.

1 Ethics, evaluation and observation: Ownership: identification with a mission? How does one 'own' an enterprise? By acting in relation to its goals (ethics), giving it value (evaluation) and objectifying it through a narrative (observation)? What is the shared narrative of an enterprise such as the CGKP (Cambridge Genetics Knowledge Park), the enthusiasm it generates (how it 'owns' people)? What could be the role of evaluators and observers ('ethnography')?

2 Incommensurability and scale, comparison: An owner: somebody with something to transact? Transacting with partners from across different technologies/commercial interests. Establishing the bases for comparisons of worth. Creating transactable goods. How far can one take the idea of trading zones? The role of commerce in evaluation.

3 Owners, authors and inventors: Owners as originators. Creativity and letting go of objects (creativity externalised). Evoking justification of origins. Copyright and patents: models of creativity. Interests in scientific authorship and recognition of collaboration and collective endeavours. Multiple employers/multiple agencies.

4 Output, accountability, and 'society' as the collaborative partner: Can one speak of owners as curators or custodians (of public values)? Collaboration turned into social investment: what is due to 'society'? Academic work, intellectual property and demands from outside. The CGKP and its publics. Responsibility and the creative role of audit. The specific need for output: recognisable deliverables.

The Stimulus of the CGKP

The Cambridge Genetics Knowledge Park will be a concrete reference point for a number of the individual questions being posed.

The CGKP has as its twin aims: 'fostering new research initiatives and collaborations and of working synergistically towards a common goal'. This vision comes from its 2001 Proposal to the Department of Health and DTI. Its expected outcomes include 'synergies from bringing together academic, clinical and industrial communities', and 'multidisciplinary research activities'. It is clear that there is an expectation of synergies across disciplines as well. One intention of the present exercise is to create an intellectual field (of discussion) and a set (or typology) of concrete studies against which to assess some of the *kinds* of synergies sparked off by the CGKP. The Proposal's anticipation that the dissemination strategy of the CGKP 'will require use of many different modalities of communication' could be applied to disciplines as well.

The advantage of focusing on interdisciplinarity is twofold. First, multidisciplinarity is taken as fundamental to research collaboration on the borders of disciplines. 'Interdisciplinarity' is the specific rubric on which most contemporary analysis about creativity and innovation in multidisciplinary research is focused. Interdisciplinarity has thus for some time been the subject of both debate and policy, and there is a depth of thinking in this area on which it will be valuable to draw. Second, interdisciplinarity will be a useful direction from which to approach a key set of conditions for the success of the CGKP. For *bringing together disciplines* is, so to speak, an internal version of the wider (external) series of collaborations envisaged in the aims. Given that the 'complexities of the modern world demand an approach that takes into account the need for pluralism, shared values, collaboration and public involvement', the Proposal strikes a note of caution: there is nothing straightforward about '*bringing together organisations* with different aims and objectives and diverse cultures'. The point about focusing on disciplines (nothing straightforward there either) is that they afford a circumscribed arena in which to lay out modes of diversity. For though communication across disciplines is necessarily built into the day-to-day practices of the CGKP, communication procedures and expected outcomes will be of many different kinds.

Working Papers

The working papers were written over the last year or two, as separate papers but overlapping in their approach to issues of interdisciplinary collaboration. The occasion of, and thus in many cases the reason for, giving the paper is noted at the end in each case. The Seminar gives a retrospective rationale for bringing them together. At the same time, it underlines their thoroughly ephemeral nature.

By demarcating collaborations across disciplines, one may be able to illuminate or differentiate other forms of collaboration too. As far as the Seminar is concerned, in setting up a series on types of ownership, it will be interesting to see what types of transactions emerge in the discussions; in turn, the conditions and expectations of emergent transactions between different parties may or may not alert one to 'new social forms' envisaged or enacted by participants. But it is bound to rehearse issues and relationships that occur over and again, in many places. Academic life is replete with antecedents, and the following papers draw attention to a few of them.

Marilyn Strathern, February 2004,
Department of Social Anthropology, Cambridge

COMPARATIVE STUDIES IN BIOTECHNOLOGY & ACCOUNTABILITY

RESEARCH GROUP IN THE THE DEPARTMENT OF SOCIAL ANTHROPOLOGY

The group brings together the overlapping interests of a number of medical and social anthropologists who have been working in the field of the new medical technologies (including reproductive technology and applications of the new genetics). Only anthropological expertise is being claimed. 'Biotechnology' and 'accountability' are both used in their common or popular sense, much as the anthropologist's way of thinking of about 'culture' and 'ethnography' has become a general possession. The group is under the overall direction of Dr Maryon McDonald.

What is *new* about these medical technologies is the way that from the outset their development has been tracked by ethical concerns, creating the field of bioethics. Bioethics has itself developed within a wider context of the audit society, of changing expectations of accountability, and of new styles of public involvement, including explicit efforts to communicate across the lay / expert divide, and across disciplines.

What is *technological* about the procedures that get so labelled is not only the way knowledge gets built into tools, but the connotations of innovation and creativity they carry. Creativity, in particular, is thought to come from unique combinations of ideas and techniques, including combinations of disciplines. Biotechnology is precisely the sign of combinatory effort. Understanding life processes and developing of techniques of exploration, notably in molecular genetics, run side by side.

What is *medical* about them is the extent to which social accountability is already programmed in through the idea of medical benefit. The justification of much work is taken to be eventual advances in human medicine. Anthropology has long made a contribution to comparative studies of illness and disease, and the regimes of their social (including medical) diagnosis and alleviation. New possibilities for comparison are suggested by technologies which find remedies in anticipation of the (diagnosis of / manifestation of) affliction. With cross-cultural comparison in the background, there are other areas that call out for anthropological observation, including what can be learnt by investigating practices 'across technologies' intended to enhance well being. The Research Group's activities encourage thinking across contexts.

ACKNOWLEDGEMENTS

Initial and emphatic thanks to James Leach for the collaborations he has brought to the Seminar, the rationale for turning these papers into a collection. Bronac Ferran and Alan Blackwell belonged to his networks in the first place. I am grateful to CRASSH for their sponsorship, and to colleagues from the CGKP for their encouragement.

In addition to individual acknowledgements, including acknowledgement of the conferences and other venues that stimulated these pieces (noted at the end of each paper), more general thanks are due. It is in giving some of these that I am brought up against just how incomplete this collection is, how unfinished its business. Of course the academic's work (there is no pretence to scholarship here) is never finished; but one of the points of 'work' is to find the appropriate limits. I have not done that in putting these pieces together. Instead, they are exposed to probably almost instant re-formulation, though there is some appropriateness in this, insofar as they belong to a world – as many have remarked – that is constantly (within some pretty gross constraints, that is) reformulating itself. A small example: the Introduction opens with an analogy between disciplines and cultures. This analogy is not so much crafted by me, let alone being anything like an analysis or a model, than a ready-made that could have been picked off an intellectual market stall, or obtained online for that matter. In the second half of 2003, the Advisory Council for Science and Technology Policy in The Hague published a report promoting multidisciplinary research, and there it is (and to the anthropologist of other places all too familiarly addressed): among 'the bottlenecks' that hinder the growth of multidisciplinary research are 'cultural difference and differences of approach between disciplines' (AWT 2003: 2 (a)).

I cite that report for another reason. It was sent to me by Emma Rothschild, herself author of a remarkable report for the UK's DTI on the Arts and Humanities in relation to Science and Technology (2001). Her personal interest has been important to this enterprise, but I give her iconic status – to stand for all those many colleagues who have contributed thoughts, ideas, references and papers. Andrew Barry, Georgina Born, Oonagh Corrigan, Sarah Green, Cori Hayden, Monica Konrad, Maryon McDonald and members of the CBA research group are among them. She is also a practitioner, and there are four practitioners in interdisciplinarity without whom the Social Property Seminar would never have been conceived or these papers materialised.

Inspiration for the topic of 'ownership' came from Bronac Ferran (Director of Interdisciplinary Arts, Arts Council England, and organiser of the 2001 CODE conference in Cambridge on intellectual property and the digital economy). Ownership is an issue that arises in all kinds of academic as well as creative contexts – and no less so in interdisciplinary endeavours that marshal different interests. She was a moving spirit behind the 2003 ACE/AHRB Fellowships that drew in Alan Blackwell (see below), building on an earlier NTAF (New Technology Arts Fellowships) scheme the previous year.

Ron Zimmern (of the Public Health Genetics Unit, Cambridge, and now Director of the University's Institute of Public Health as well as Founder-Director of the CGKP) provided an impetus for the Seminar from his interest in the phenomenon of 'multiple agencies', the combinations of funding, employment and secondment that make up each research node, bringing together persons, relationships and interests in a 'motivated' fashion. Interests may or may not be aligned with disciplines, but point to the way people attach themselves to ('own') projects, and to what they hope to realise as values ('own') for themselves.

While individual IDWs follow the Colloquia in order to pick up a theme for development, the models will come from experimental associations between creative artists and scientists, and are supported by an unusual collaboration between the Arts and Humanities Research Board and the Arts Council England, and from industrial design. Here the genius belongs to Alan Blackwell, from the Computer Laboratory, co-founder of Crucible, the Cambridge-based network for research in interdisciplinary design.

Finally, if Helga Nowotny (Collegium Helveticum, Swiss Federal Institute of Technology [ETH], Zurich), and her colleagues had not laid out so clearly and critically some of the conditions of modern knowledge production, there would have been no starting place. Among her notable practical contributions, 2003 also saw the launch of the Branco-Weiss Fellowship Programme in 'Society in Science', which is a model of interdisciplinary innovation at its most open.

REFERENCES

AWT [Adviesraad voor het Wetenschaps-en Technologiebeleid] 2003 *I + 1 > 2 [One plus One is more than Two]: Promoting Multidisciplinary Research*, The Hague: AWT.

DTI (Department of Trade and Industry) 2001 *Imagination and Understanding: Report on the Arts and Humanities in relation to Science and Technology*, London: Council for Science and Technology.

INTRODUCTION

In Crisis Mode

A Comment on Interculturality

> The main theoretical focus of anthropology must be on the
> dynamics of interculturality at different levels of magnitude.
> (Lourdes Arizpe 1996: 97)

Professor Arizpe has underlined the need for social science,
particularly my own discipline, social anthropology, to come to
grips with the non-linear nature of social phenomena.

> The cultural and social phenomena we are witnessing
> [today] ... are unprecedented in human history for ... rea-
> sons [including] ... the levels of complexity they involve....
> The main theoretical focus of anthropology must be on the
> dynamics of interculturality at different levels of magni-
> tude (Arizpe 1996: 89, 97).

I approach recent advances in the social sciences through
the dynamics of interculturality – not across societies or ethnic
groups, but across disciplines. Interculturality I take to mean
the condition of our already inhabiting one another's cultures.[1]
Even more visible than the divides between different social
science disciplines have been efforts to build bridges between
the social sciences and the arts and humanities on the one
hand, and the natural sciences on the other. By its very nature,
this bridging work resists linear definition. It contributes to
present day perceptions of complexity.

If it is impossible to speak generally on behalf of all the
social sciences, it is certainly possible to point to some very
general conditions that have, over the last 50 years, given rise

to parallel perceptions that we live in an increasingly complex world. I refer to the role that *crises* have played in the development of disciplines. Crises in human affairs have a particular impact in social science because of its orientation (amongst others) to response-mode investigation. There are issues of enormous interest here for anyone concerned with policy, and especially research policy.

Bluntly put, one way in which the social sciences 'advance' is in response to current issues, especially when couched in terms of public concern. These are moments that present themselves as requiring attention, whether or not they were on any else's agenda before. I am thinking less of catastrophes – natural disasters, famine, warfare, the displacement of persons – than of issues that may have been in the making for some time, and then suddenly gather momentum. The point is that when they come to a head, that is, when they seem imperative to study, one must gather what tools there are to hand to deal with them. Methods and theories devised for other purposes have to be pressed into service. At the same time, a situation may be presented as a crisis precisely because of its widely ramifying (and unforeseen) effects. Part of difficulty with the problem may be that it has developed from the coming together of diverse circumstances, and may require several different approaches to deal with it (Calhoun 2002). Indeed, such situations are often identifiable by the *multi-* or *interdisciplinary nature* of the expertise they seem to summon.

In addition to interdisciplinarity, crises generate two further conditions. First, even though the crisis as such may lie in the very unpredictability of events, responding to or dealing with one after another leads to a sense of *anticipation*. It is as though crises could not only be imagined but be dealt with (Hayden 2002) ahead of time. One extremely significant development, across the board of social science enquiry, touches on research regulation, which in the UK includes the rise of 'bioethics' – at once an arena for reflection and a monitoring instrument – and ELSI. 'ELSI' is the attempt to think simultaneously about the ethical, legal and social implications of the outcomes of research in advance of its conduct.

This shades into the second condition, which comes from the fact that by their nature, crises are threatening. We try to prevent them, to *pre-empt* the lethal chain of cause and effect – and like the followers of millenarian movements may react by imposing regulations and rules upon ourselves to avert disaster (Barry 2001). So we have regulation for researchers and crisis-avoidance for governments, as in the protocols developed to deal with embryo experimentation. New practices of accountability monitor investigations involving 'human subjects'. New practices of audit demand that organisations know how to describe – more than that, to do social analyses of – themselves. Reflexivity and self-referentiality have become bywords of organisational cultures and research cultures alike.

I suggest that these concerns have had a profound effect on the shaping of social science, effects that have particularly gained momentum in the latter part of that 50 year period.

Interdisciplinarity

I continue to find useful Callon's (1998) contrast between hot and cold to delineate changing pressures on the way in which knowledge is used, and rehearse his points again (cf. Strathern 2002). In 'cold' situations, calculated decisions can be taken on the basis of relatively stable measurements of outcomes. He instances the pollution of a watercourse by a chemical factory: sensors are already calibrated, analytical procedures codified, experts know how to do the calculations. 'Hot' situations, by contrast, arise from the unpredictable interaction of diverse factors, as in the 'turmoil' of BSE, where an apparently isolated calculation (to save money by reducing the temperature for processing animal feeds) led to wide-scale havoc. By turns, as he says (1998: 260–1), public inquiry had to involve vets, farmers, manufacturers of animal feed, proponents of deregulation, beefburgers, outraged members of the public, the media, prions, butchers, transporters, and so on.[2]

Unforeseen chains of events are commonplace; 'heat' comes from the mix of quite different orders of knowledge, including that drawn from non-specialists. The scientist cannot remain in his laboratory, but has to engage both with other specialists and non-specialists, of all kinds, for 'society as a whole must agree to take action' (1998: 262). A network of diverse interests, policies and research outcomes somehow have to be combined, and instruments of calculation and measurement have to be created and agreed upon as fast as calculations are required. Hot situations, he argues, are becoming increasingly prevalent as controversies cross boundaries of discipline and skill, and it gets increasingly hard to cool them down, that is, produce consensus on how to measure what. But such situations, registered routinely in information overload,[3] are also commonplace within the research process and its application. The result is interlocking, scale-crossing complexity. Social scientists are as much caught up in this as anyone.

Some obvious fields of enquiry come to mind. Public debate over the propriety of assisted conception techniques has raged since the birth of the first IVF child in 1978, and continues nearly a quarter century on with the debates about stem cell research ('cloning'). Social scientists studying this field find themselves in the company of ethicists, genetic counsellors and clinicians. An audit culture stimulated by increasing protocols on 'research with human subjects', in the context of which, social scientists find themselves in the company of accountants and administrators, increases the pressure on primary research. These concerns crossover into the legal area of intellectual property. Property debates are stimulated by the new genetics and, with the decoding of the human genome, by the race to patent 'genes'; here social scientists find themselves in the company of geneticists, lawyers and ethicists. Such debates are further fanned by public controversy over copyright to computer and music programmes, where social scientists and lawyers find themselves in the company of scientific and literary authors. When it comes to cultural and intellectual property in developing countries over the last decade, stimulated by the World Trade Organisation (WTO), the World Intellectual Property Organisation (WIPO) and the United Nations 'Decade of Indigenous Peoples', social scientists must engage with activists and Non-Governmental Organisations, as well as the natural scientists, developers and resource managers concerned with environment and biodiversity following the two Earth Summits. Obviously the list could go on. But the point is that any such situation can fuel a sense of 'having to do something'. This may be compounded when 'Society' is appealed to as an arbiter, and the social scientist is called in to represent the 'social' view. No one person, no one discipline, could grasp all the dimensions.

There is a particular issue here, to do with the way that social science, imagined as speaking for Society, gets linked up to (say) natural science and a more general issue of interdisciplinarity as a phenomenon of crisis-response. These are themselves examples of complex interfacing. For social science moves into these new fields not so much as a result of internal policy making, that is, as an outcome of its own theory-driven questions, but rather as an outcome of its largely responsive mode. It will draw on existing theories and findings, and turn them to new use. And that in turn is partly an *effect* of interdisciplinarity. In a many-disciplined context, each expert becomes a representative of his or her discipline. Indeed, experts will be turned to for their 'traditional' knowledge, for specialist wisdom assumed to be already in place. In such circumstances, internal debate between experts (referring back to the arguments through which different models of knowledge are contested and established) are often looked upon at best as a distraction, and at worst as disciplinary in-fighting or self-indulgence at the expense of public need.

At the same time there is a need to conserve the division of labour between disciplines, if only because the value of a discipline is precisely in its ability to account for its conditions of existence and thus as to how it arrives at its knowledge practices. In such circumstances, social scientists might want to think rather carefully about, for instance, just how they are to speak for 'Society'.

Anticipation

Dealing with a crisis is one thing; being in a state of readiness for the next is another. Anticipation has its own effects. Here I turn to a kind of routine crisis in the pursuit of knowledge, which is how to deal with the unforeseen – normal in the life of social systems, a 'crisis' for those who claim to know how to know about them, that is, the social systems. Yet the unpredictable would seem the least likely thing one could anticipate. This is where social anthropology can make a contribution to social science at large.

What research strategy could possibly collect information on unpredictable outcomes? Social anthropology has one trick up its sleeve: the deliberate attempt to generate more data than the investigator is aware of at the time of collection. Anthropologists deploy open-ended, non-linear methods of data collection which they call ethnography;[4] I refer particularly to the nature of ethnography entailed in anthropology's version of fieldwork (Arizpe 1996: 91). Rather than devising research protocols that will purify the data in advance of analysis, the anthropologist embarks on a participatory exercise which yields materials for which analytical protocols are often devised after the fact. In the field the ethnographer may work by indirection, creating tangents from which the principal subject can be observed (through 'the wider social context'). But what is tangent at once stage may become central at next.

One example of a crisis in the making has already been mentioned; its genesis falls at the 25 year dividing line since the founding of the International Social Science Council (ICSS, an NGO in formal association with UNESCO). Throughout the 1960s and into the 1970s most family research in the UK had focused on households, issues of upbringing, poverty and welfare, and so forth, and had been largely the province of non-anthropologists. There were one or two anthropologists who were interested in family networks, and in the way in which, especially in rural areas, families 'belonged' to particular locales in rural areas (e.g. Cohen 1982), but the subject seemed to many no more than a byway. Then assisted conception broke onto the scene – helping the infertile to 'complete their families', creating stranger donors, questioning what made a mother or a father. And almost straight away the public imagination extended the social possibilities: parents and children could gift fertility across the generations, having 'biological' children was released from conventions of heterosexuality, maternal ageing was a barrier newly surmountable. A crisis of propriety for the regulators turned into a crisis of interpretation for the researcher. What kinds of families were now being created? Anthropology offered two research routes.

First, at the outset it was able to draw on theorising already in place. This was theorising not about 'families' as such, but about 'kinship'; not about the institutional form, but about the nature of relationships set up through procreative practices. It had vast comparative experience, from across many societies, of the way people deal with conception, the values they put on relatedness through social and biological ties, and so forth. A case of turning to tools ready at hand, anthropology could draw on existing models in conceptualising new combinations of social relations (Edwards *et al.* 1993).

Second, previous ethnographic studies in the UK were able to provide a cultural context of sorts. That apparently unpromising work on networks and families belonging to particular locales obviously could not have predicted the New

Reproductive Technologies (NRTs), but it did provide a resource for understanding people's reactions. The promises and threats offered by the new technologies were new for the public too, and people were told so, as diverse reactions were turned into an epistemological and ethical crisis by the media ('what do we know and what are we to think?'). But some interesting antecedents of people's attitudes and values were recoverable. Indeed, in one notable instance in the UK (Edwards 2000), an earlier study of local families, in this case within an urban milieu, turned out to be crucial for understanding their later reactions as members of the public. These people readily discussed questions of identity and belonging posed by the NRTs, and where the boundaries should be drawn. The crisis they saw looming was about incest and inbreeding, and the boundary question was fuelled by the way families were regarded as 'rooted' in places. Seemingly irrelevant byways in anthropological research turned out to contain information highly relevant to what – to most people, including ordinary social scientists – had been an unforeseen medical and clinical development.

We may speak of anticipation by default, to be found in tools already there or in open-ended modes of study, such as 'ethnography', which allow one to recover the antecedents of future crises from material not collected for the purpose. If one were to formalise it, then it would be to anticipate a future need to know something that cannot be defined in the present.[5] But, moving away from anthropology and turning to the wider picture again, we see how anticipation can also become routinised, and how the possibilities of research could get closed down rather than opened up.

Pre-emption

In the UK a new epistemic 'uncertainty' accompanies an institutionalised uncertainty as to how far one can trust public service agencies (as well as company directors). This creates and is created by ever more attempts to check up on them (O'Neill 2002). Let me cross disciplinary fields for a moment. What has been happening in science holds interest for social science.

The number of 'science and society' initiatives set up in recent years across Europe testify to the importance of the relationship.[6] Now a widespread consensus that we live in an

'age of uncertainty' has become the newly explicit environment
to this relationship. The phrase is from Nowotny *et al.*'s (2001)
sequel to *The New Production of Knowledge* (Gibbons *et al.*
1994), which explored the difference between two modes (1 and
2) of knowledge production. Uncertainty is not a passive state:
as a precondition for innovation (Barnett 2000), it is animated
by, among other things, society's internalisation of science.

> In traditional [modern] society science was 'external' ...
> and scientists saw their task as the benign reconstitution
> of society according to 'modern' principles [Mode 1].... In
> contemporary [modern] society, in contrast, science is
> 'internal'; as a result science and research are no longer
> terminal or authoritative projects ... but instead, by creat-
> ing new knowledge, they add fresh elements of uncertainty
> and instability [Mode 2] (Nowotny *et al.* 2001: 2)

Now, Mode 2 knowledge production accompanies 'an
important shift in the regime of control ...[whereby] control is
now exercised indirectly and from the "inside" ... [through] ever
more elaborate systems of peer review, more formal quality
control systems, and other forms of audit, assessment and
evaluation' (Nowotny *et al.* 2001: 115). Audit gets globally
dispersed (across sectors of society and across societies)
through its appeal as an internal mechanism of self-
improvement.

The academy continues to have a major role in the
production of science, and in the UK alongside audit of the
institution has come a kind of 'knowledge audit' (my phrase).
Here the examination system has returned in a gross way to
haunt the auditing of university affairs, a devotion to paper has
blossomed into the necessity of paper trails for everything, and
accountability becomes at once increasingly difficult to
discharge (more elaborate systems of audit) and increasingly
easy (routinised). One result is that satisfaction with the
accounting process becomes harder to sustain (Power 1997). In
short, as more energy becomes tied up in the routinisation of
procedures, less becomes available for spending on 'real'
accountability. As for the creative authorship of scholars,
Biagioli (2000) has noted the emergent conventions by which
scientific periodicals try to recognise 'everyone' involved in a
piece of research, while avoiding being swamped by multi-
authorship citations, an 'inflation of authorship credit'. Level of

activity may not be accompanied by a concomitant rise in a sense of overall benefit. To take the last example, multi-authored works: these exist within a dynamic of inflation (the more one is cited the less each citation counts) against inertia (more and more resources are bound up in keeping the activity going – making sure everyone's name is there).[7]

Checks on the delivery of knowledge, as through the UK's four yearly national Research Assessment Exercise, are one thing; input (research funding) and output (publications, patents) offer indicators that the academic community is delivering. Checks on the nature of knowledge are another. For here monitoring reaches beyond the point of production to consumption, to the point at which information about something becomes knowledge for someone. Partly because of the scale of public investment, science has come under particular scrutiny. In the conventional view, its effectiveness is mediated through products, as when technology is harnessed to engineering or pharmaceuticals. But the last 25 years have seen an increasing supposition that the public should *understand* (absorb knowledge of) science, or at least understand the science agenda, that is, its aims and objectives. While Nowotny *et al.* (2001: 240) relegate need for the 'public understanding of science' to traditional aims (Mode 1), their following comment sketches in some of the Mode 2 complexity: the realisation that more information does not necessarily lead to more empathy – rather, education encourages critical questioning, for example on the traditional distinction between experts and laypeople. It is in this context that 'science and society' burgeons as a rubric for research funding programmes.[8]

Science's orientation to 'society' has moved from (a) demonstrating its effectiveness in reaching potential consumers, through the promise of (say) medical advancement; to (b) requiring something like endorsement from society itself. Here consumption becomes part of the production process. In research policy rhetoric: the switch away from 'public understanding' of science to 'public engagement' entails a switch from society as the passive consumer to society as an active consumer-participant in knowledge production. The science that was once robust through its own validation procedures (Mode 1) must now acquire an(other) efficacy from beyond itself (Mode 2). Insofar as society can confer acceptability, and can take on an auditing role, scientific knowledge makes itself robust in being seen to be 'socially robust' (Gibbons 1999). In effect, science incorporates society into its aims and objectives in order to pre-empt society's verdict.

Conclusion: Already Intercultural

Beyond the regulation of 'good practice' implicit in audit is an emergent cultural value, 'quality', and a new social phenomenon, professionals devoted to quality control (Munro and Mouritisen 1996; Miller 2003). Good practice is at once taken as evidence of itself, and perceived as a layer added to others. Audit carries its own double resonance of ethical behaviour and effective action: propriety and good financial management merge standards of measurement with targets for policy action. It has become a global phenomenon (Strathern 2000). Power (1994: 36–7) gives a lead: 'What is audited is whether there is a system which embodies standards and the standards of performance themselves are shaped by the need to be auditable ... audit become a formal 'loop' by which the system *observes itself*. 'Audit is an emerging principle of social organization, ... a major shift of power ... from teachers, engineers and managers to overseers' (1994: 47).[9] This process promotes self-management, where 'the manager ... gets internalised: externally imposed control becomes internally generated motivation' (Martin 1997: 241). What is true for management becomes true for the kind of knowledge people hold, and which a social scientist might also wish to know.

For one consequence of this inter-folding of expectations is already evident in certain types of investigation. Anthropologists once regarded it their job to elicit reflexivity from their research subjects, but nowadays they are often presented with a high degree of already cultivated self-awareness and self-consciousness (members of these organisations reflecting on their own positions); presented with what one might call indigenous social analysis (internal interest in analysing the structure and role of the organisation); and presented with a desire to engage with the social environment in a responsive mode (openly advocating learning) – all of which can be put into the complexity language of self-referentiality (the way social systems describe themselves and absorb information about themselves into their operations).[10] When specifically social anthropological models and tools are co-opted (Wright and Nelson 1997), the effects of such an (often welcomed) appropriation must in turn rebound on social anthropology as a discipline.[11]

Out of this comes a social sensibility, familiar at least to the anthropological fieldworker. Where research involves 'human subjects', researcher and subject are likely to *share* problems. One striking set of problems frequently held in common is information overload, which is an outcome not only of enhanced communications through information technology, but also of these very social practices of iterative communications and self-reference. This brings me to a concluding question. What does it mean to produce information for educational and policy purposes in an increasingly complex and information-saturated world alongside (UNESCO and other) practitioners who have very concrete applications and needs in mind? Do we have to go into crisis mode in order to answer the question?

NOTES

Acknowledgement: Many thanks are due to Lourdes Arizpe, not just for this conference (and the kind invitation) but for her anthropological voice at UNESCO.

1 And at all levels of social interaction. Through its regular World Education, Science, Culture and Information Reports, UNESCO has played a role in steering international policy and intellectual trends towards cultural policies and interdisciplinary 'system thinking'. One may add that through the International Social Science Council, Man and the Biosphere and Management of Social Transformations programmes, UNESCO has specifically facilitated the emergence of complexity thinking from a co-evolution between the natural and social sciences by (for example) re-incorporating human dimensions into cybernetic climate change models.

2 'The controversy lurches first one way and the other – because nothing is certain, neither the knowledge base nor the methods of measurement' (1998: 261).

3 Overload because different sources of information are non-reducible (non-assimilable) to one another – there is not one but a multiplicity of *fundamental* frameworks.

4 'Ethnography' is now an established method in many contexts that owe little to any influence from social anthropology.

5 Communications technologies seem to increase the gap between control and goal attainment: 'everything now is a possible object of communication' (Luhmann 1990: 105), leaving 'nothing equivalent to the silent efficiency of what once seemed sufficient: truth'. Anthropological observation has another 'silent efficiency' to it: outcomes not anticipated in study protocols, the surprise of contingency (Battaglia 1999), descriptions not to be elicited from the subjects themselves – in short, *where self-knowledge cannot help.*

And that is partly because society as such can never itself be a system (see Law 1994).

6 The following comes from M. Strathern (forthcoming).

7 Here I take Brennan's deployment of 'inertia' as the binding of energy at fixed points in ways which drive up the real cost of production. She applies it to the circulation of commodities, the way for example in which the cost of commodities are only kept down because of the ever increasing applications of technology in production and marketing (2000: 11). Notably, in agriculture this occurs when applications such as pesticides and fertilisers become perpetually bound to the productive operation.

8 The title which the British House of Lords gave to its enquiry into public perceptions of science (Franklin 2001: 339–40).

9 Self-referential systems may observe themselves; organisations in an audit society become *users* of descriptions of themselves. Added to what 'the system' is doing in its own communications is the meta-communication of people's self-descriptions: reflexivity under the prospect of audit sustains a judgmental self (Hoskin 1995, Munro 1999). In the hands of social planners, such reflexivity can become a literal aim or objective. Higher Education audit thus offers an arena in which to follow through Tsoukas's (1994) observations about the turn from social engineering to reflective management with insights from complexity theory, e.g. 'They may try reflexive planning, taking into account reactions to their own activity. But, in fact, they can only write and rewrite the memories of the system, using simplistic devices which they necessarily invalidated by their own activity' (Luhmann 1990: 180). The planners' dilemma applies to educational auditors. One cannot simply use complexity theory to engineer better systems of control.

10 All social organisations have complex features, but a particular kind of analysis is demanded by organisations which not only do their own 'ethnography' (describe themselves) but absorb such knowledge into their policies: they become literally 'self-referential'. Contemporary examples abound, e.g. in the international arena of NGOs, here sometimes in dialogue with concepts derived directly from anthropology (Riles 2000). What are the implications of adding the observer's further layer of description to organisations that absorb descriptions as prescriptions for practice?

11 Ingrid Putkonen's doctoral dissertation ('The global subject: a study of a family planning NGO, globalisation and the shaping of subjectivity', Cambridge, 2001) analyses a participatory education project in Mexico from this point of view.

REFERENCES

Arizpe L. (ed) 1996 *Cultural Dimensions of Global Change: An Anthropological Account*, UNESCO.

Barnett, R. 2000 *Realizing the University in an Age of Supercomplexity*, Buckingham: Society for Research into Higher Education & Open University Press

Barry, A. 2001 *Political Machines: Governing a Technological Society*, London: Athlone Press.

Battaglia D. 1999 'Towards an ethics of the open subject: anthropology and contingency', in H. Moore (ed.), *Anthropological Theory Today*, Cambridge: Polity.

Biagioli, M. 2000 'Right or rewards? Changing contexts and definitions of scientific authorship', *Journal of College and University Law* 27: 83–108.

Brennan, T. 2000 *Exhausting Modernity: Grounds for a New Economy*, London: Routledge.

Calhoun, C. 2002 'Introduction to roundtable on rethinking International Studies in a global context', *Items & Issues (U.S. Social Science Research Council)* 3: 1–4.

Callon, M. 1998 'An essay on framing and overflowing: economic externalities revisited by sociology', in M. Callon (ed.), *The Laws of the Markets*, Oxford: Blackwell Publishers/The Sociological Review.

Cohen, A.P. (ed.) 1982 *Belonging: Identity and Social Organisation in British Rural Cultures*, Manchester: Manchester University Press.

Edwards, J. 2000 *Born and Bred: Idioms of Kinship and New Reproductive Technologies in England*, Oxford: Oxford University Press.

Edwards, J., Franklin, S., Hirsch, E., Price, F. and Strathern, M. 1993 *Technologies of Procreation: Kinship in the Age of Assisted Conception*, Manchester University Press. (2nd edn, London: Routledge, 1999.)

Franklin, S. 2001 'Culturing biology: cell lines for the second millennium', *Health* 5: 335–54.

Gibbons, M. 1999 'Science's new social contract with society', *Nature* 402 (Supplement) C81–4.

Gibbons, M., Limoges, C., Nowotny, H., Schwartzman, S., Scott, P., and Trow, M. 1994 *The New Production of Knowledge: The Dynamics of Science and Research in Contemporary Society*, London: Sage Publications.

Hayden, C. 2002 'Towards an ethnography of the adverse effect', Paper delivered at EASA conference, for panel 'Genes, Genomes, and Genetics', convenor G. Pálsson, Copenhagen.

Hoskin K. 1995 'The viewing self and the world we view', *Organization* 2: 141–62.

Law J. 1984 *Organizing Modernity*, Oxford: Blackwell.

Luhmann N. 1990 *Essays on Self-reference*, New York: Columbia University Press.

Martin, E. 1997 'Managing Americans: policy and changes in the meanings of work and the self', in C. Shore and S. Wright (eds), *Anthropology of Policy*, London: Routledge.

Miller, D. 2003 'The virtual moment', *Journal of the Royal Anthrop. Institute* 9: 57–75.

Munro, R. 1999 'The cultural performance of control', *Organization Studies* 20: 619–40.

Munro R. and Mouritsen J. (eds) 1996 *Accountability: Power, Ethos and the Technologies of Managing*, London: Thomson Business Press.

Nowotny, H., Scott, P. and Gibbons, M. 2001 *Re-Thinking Science: Knowledge and the Public in an Age of Uncertainty*, Oxford: Polity.

O'Neill, O. 2002 *A Question of Trust* [BBC Reith Lectures], Cambridge: Cambridge University Press.

Power M. 1994 *The Audit Explosion*, London: Demos.

——— 1997 *The Audit Society: Rituals of Verification*, Oxford: Oxford University Press.

Putkonen, I. 2001 'The global subject: a study of a family planning NGO, globalisation and the shaping of subjectivity', doctoral dissertation, Dept. Social Anthropology, Cambridge.

Riles A. 2000 *The Network Inside Out*, Ann Arbor: University of Michigan Press.

Strathern, M. (ed.) 2000 *Audit Cultures: Anthropological Studies in Accountability, Ethics and the Academy*, London: Routledge.

——— 2002 'Externalities in comparative guise', *Economy & Society* 31: 250–67 (spec. issue 'The technological economy', (eds) A. Barry and D. Slater.

——— [forthcoming] 'Robust knowledge and fragile futures', in Aihwa Ong and Stephen Collier (eds) *Global Assemblages: Technology, Politics and Ethics*, Oxford: Blackwells.

Tsoukas H. (ed.) 1994 *New Thinking in Organisational Behaviour: From Social Engineering to Reflective Action*, Oxford: Butterworth.

Wright, S and N Nelson 1997 *Power and Participatory Development: Theory and Practice*, London: IT.

From: ISSC & UNESCO International conference on 'Social Science and Social Policy in 21st century', Vienna, December 2002. Plenary session 'Advances in Social and Behavioural Science Disciplines' convened by Lourdes Arizpe. An earlier version of this paper has appeared in the proceedings, Leszek A. Kosiński and Kurt Pawlik (eds) 2003, *Social Science at the Crossroads: Proceedings if the International Conference on Social Science and Social Policy in the 21st Century*, Paris, International Social Science Council. Permission to reproduce is gratefully acknowledged.

WORKING PAPER ONE

Knowledge on its Travels

Dispersal and Divergence in the Make-up of Communities

What makes a 'community'? The question becomes interesting in inter-institutional or inter-disciplinary contexts premised on the creative mix of expertise from diverse locations. Knowledge comes from, and is drawn into, different organisational structures. At the same time, the notion that knowledge travels (across locations) invites one to reconstruct communities in its wake, tracing connections after the fact. Late twentieth and early twenty-first century citizens of the knowledge economy, inspired by electronic circuitry, also see sense in *planning* knowledge communities, imagining connections-to-be. This Working Paper explores certain models of knowledge dispersal in order to ask a local question: what kind of 'community' might the newly established Cambridge Genetics Knowledge Park be generating.

There is a fascinating experiment in the organisation of knowledge being carried out at the moment in the University of Cambridge. It is on a large scale. There are many ways of counting its elements, for the units can not only be variably clumped, but also jump levels of organisational complexity. The intention of the experiment is to bring together expertise that is lodged in bodies of diverse kinds. To give you some idea, these are named[1] variously as *faculties, departments, research centres, research groups, research programmes, units, institutes, schools* (as in School of Humanities and Social

Sciences) and *laboratories*, all largely embedded within the University, across some 17 *disciplines* and areas of *expertise*, but drawing in allies from external *institutes, resources centres* and *units*, including a *campus,* as well as collaboration with the University of East Anglia, while outreach to industry brings in other entities, such as an *enterprise* (as in 'programme'), a regional *initiative,* and a transatlantic *company;* there are in addition named *participants, partners* and *sponsors,* and, more diffusely, *consumers* and *the public.* 'Organisation' is itself represented in the core staff under a *director,* a *supervisory board* and an *executive board.* Now all these bodies[2] have people attached, though individuals can obviously occupy more than one social space. So what kind of community, or communities, will be forming under this impetus?

Of course it is easy in a networked society to extrapolate 'connections' of all kinds, but this particular conglomeration is composed of specific and locatable links between people. Moreover, they all think of themselves, from its perspective, as part of a single venture. The venture concerns generating a particular kind of knowledge from knowledge that already exists or is in the making. What is interesting in the present circumstances is that this vision doesn't just require the organisation of knowledge, it is *about* the organisation of knowledge. Its first remit is to 'establish an administrative structure that will actively and explicitly bring together the activities of academic research with those of the commercial sector, clinical and public health practice, and the views of both consumers of genetic services and the public', the purpose of the second being to 'create knowledge (which we define as information that has been validated through critical appraisal of research findings, and integrated with an ethical, legal and social analysis and the input of consumer views)' (Zimmern 2001: 1). The focus is human genetics, and I refer of course to the Cambridge Genetics Knowledge Park (CGKP).

I shall write a little about the CGKP itself at the end of this Working Paper, but most of my account will be of other places. In fact it is important that it is about other places. Because what I am in search of is how to *approach* the CGKP anthropologically, this ethnographic object, this virtual city. From which gate should I enter? One way is to think about one of its assumptions: that when people produce knowledge with other kinds of people in mind, as participants will be doing when they are wearing their CGKP hats, they hope that – like a transferable skill – the knowledge will travel.[3] It doesn't have to look the same at the end of its journey, but it should have been on a recognisable journey. The question then becomes what makes knowledge (able to) travel. There are some obvious answers, but there are also some very interesting, if less obvious, routes to take.

Preamble

How is knowledge transmitted from one kind of community to another – and what happens to such knowledge when it travels?[4] Perhaps we can make the question an interesting one with which to think about communities.[5] What can we infer about communities from the way in which knowledge travels?

I find myself drawing on several different kinds of placements, which may or may not be geographically locatable. Indeed in some senses my account will resemble little more than an accumulation of examples, a primitive cataloguing, an unordered archive even. For I do not wish to pre-judge *where* we might find 'communities'. I am happy to include circuits, networks, relations of all kinds. And if a community is identifiable in contexts where practices of communication create recognisable purposes and intelligible values, these are of course the preconditions for competition as well as cooperation. My particular purpose is to think about the communities that knowledge creates when the kind of knowledge we are dealing with is explicitly on the move.[6] Of course, we never actually see the movement – what we stop to describe is at rest itself; however many places it has come from, we give it a singular location in the moment of reflection. So I am driven back to looking at *markers* of mobility. I take up two.

The *first* is to do with how knowledge is rendered portable, and by rendering I mean the way that a commodity, for example, is a product rendered exchangeable on the market. However, I leave out of this account practices of exchange, negotiation and transaction, not to speak of 'trading zones' (see postscript to Working Paper Two) and all those situations where commonality is created during the course of transactions.[7] I focus instead on production, on how knowledge is produced in a form amenable to travel, export, wandering; if looking back on the process of transmission one discerns communities of producers in its wake, the form in which they have rendered knowledge portable will perhaps tell us something about them in turn.

The *second* marker of mobility is found in practices of consumption, where it is mobility itself which is being consumed, since what is valued about knowledge is that it can be communicated. An interesting and recent phenomenon here are intended communities: when it is the consumer's actual goal to create circuits of communication. Largely left out of the account are questions of audience, partly because fuller treatment would entail discriminating between knowledge and information. (As it is, the focus is on situations where we can talk of knowledge as information brought within the personal organisation of the consumer in a way that transforms how they recognise or think about things.) I take situations where the consumer is in turn valued for the ability to at once absorb things from elsewhere and pass them further on.

It will be obvious that the general context in which I am talking is Euro-American. I draw from concrete examples on which we have ethnographic reports, but must repeat that there is nothing comprehensive about my diverse models. While the paper has an overall narrative impetus, the links between the parts are not logical or structural, and the order could have been in any direction. Moreover, the elements I distribute *across* the different sections of the paper could all, more or less, be excavated from *within* one of the examples. My aim is very simple: to set out some of the ways in which knowledge is carried. Particular carriers point to particular communities created in the process.

Production: Making Knowledge Mobile

Here are some – out of myriad – examples of knowledge being rendered portable.

1 The product

Knowledge that goes into the making of something travels with the product itself. This is how we commonly think of *technology*: know-how embedded in the artefact. When it is a product manufactured for the market, the price one pays includes the price of the knowledge, whatever went into the research and development (R & D). We encounter this in a very explicit form in the philosophy behind patents – patents allow those who carried out the R & D to assert rights over how the knowledge will be used by other manufacturers. But whereas other manufacturers may be interested in this knowledge, in some cases literally taking a product apart to see how it is made, the consumer doesn't have to absorb it as knowledge of this kind (that is, knowledge about the productive process): they want to be told the results of its use. An example is the anti-cancer drug Taxol (Goodman and Walsh 2001). The dispensers and recipients of the drug are only interested in the specification of its properties insofar as these indicate its likely effects.

If we are looking for a community inscribed in a product, it has to be the community of producers. It is rather extending the term to see everyone caught up in the manufacturing process as a community, but we might legitimately use the term to refer to those who *collaborated* in producing the knowledge base. This will have involved a composite of actors. Traces of some of this composite will be in the patent specifications (if patents are taken out), which name the inventors. The 'inventors' are of course those who produced the knowledge (of chemical properties, say) in the form that could be used in the design of the product. Knowledge of those properties may have travelled in other forms. Taxol is notorious here. Developed initially in the States with public money, Taxol was first investigated as a natural product (bark from the Pacific Yew) but the knowledge ended up as a formula for a chemical compound, and the private manufacturing company that eventually brought it to the market patented a semi-synthetic product which did not use the tree at all.[8]

A patent is itself a device for enabling knowledge to travel; the theory at least is that it encourages the first developers of the product to try to get it to the market, knowing that the knowledge is at once public and secure for a while. It also encourages 'inventing around', since the public knowledge can be drawn on, under license, for other products. But you may well object that the beneficiaries of intellectual property claims indicate a very truncated 'community'. Indeed, the truncated nature of such credit has been contrasted with other forms of accreditation which point more fully to communities of producers.

A *publication* is the academic's product par excellence. In the case of scientific publications (Biagioli and Galison 2003) the individual shares findings with the scientific community at large, so that knowledge taken out of a public domain is returned to it. Biagioli (2000) sees this as a crucial distinction between the reward system and IPR.[9] The reward system recognises that individuals also carry responsibility for what they contribute: 'scientific responsibility is not a legal category, but a set of relations among colleagues' (2000: 104). How those relations are conveyed in the citations that accompany the work is a complex and often fraught matter. It is common to find whole congeries of participants in the research process as named authors, and in a short paper the credits may take up much of the text. The interest for us here is twofold. First, the act of publication – in a book, journal or whatever – is an explicit attempt to launch or float knowledge; second, at the very point when knowledge – and the observation relates to conventions in scientific publishing – is set off on its travels, its genesis within a community of sorts is spelled out name by name.

That description in turn may well be a limited one. Even where multiple authorship is acknowledged, not all the authors may be equally visible to one another (obscured by the differences of expertise), and non-authorial producers may be out of sight altogether. There are other contexts where inventors and producers are not publicly visible as authors at all. Gusterson (2003: 300) describes the reticence of nuclear scientists: '[A]lthough some knowledge circulates in formally authored texts, much of it circulates orally or via informal publications such as memos and reports'; collaborating in teams down-plays individual citations and knowledge is not free to travel beyond the confines of the laboratory.[10] It is no surprise that there are different circuits and spheres that delimit degrees of mobility. Clearly the kinds of communities formed by the circulation of knowledge in the course of producing an artefact, a product, can only be imperfectly gleaned from the product itself. So let's go back a stage – to the actual site of the creation of the product, to the point at which everyone is working together, and the outcome is still in the future. Knowledge distributed across several fields links them (those working together) in chains of communication. The second kind of knowledge-carrier I want to talk about is the project.

2 The project

This offers a seemingly obvious example of how one kind of community forms, namely round a venture still in the making, such as a *research programme*. Although people may come from heterogeneous backgrounds (different disciplines, different expertises), the project gives their contributions a focus. Here, then, knowledge is not made mobile by being launched on a wider world as a patent or a publication; on the contrary what makes it mobile is that those with the project-goal in view create a world of their own. Knowledge is meant to circulate among all those who contribute to the programme. That is not the same as making it collective or public within the organisation, and people may put up numerous barriers between themselves. If we are looking at what creates mobility, what is germane is the way in which experts among themselves assume an object of common interest that predisposes them to give credence and value to the different kinds of knowledge being brought to the table.[11] Such expertise may not uncontested (indeed contest may crucial to validation), but the axiom is that it becomes relevant to know what others know in order (among other things) to keep track of what is happening to 'the project' itself.[12] It is found in all kind of 'problem-solving' orientations to knowledge acquisition (Schön 1991).

A sobering reflection on such an axiom, however, is Law's (2002) account of a massive UK government-funded 'project' that failed after years of work, and – by contrast with Taxol[13]– where the failure of the project may well have dispersed much of its accumulated knowledge into other projects (it was used elsewhere), but caused the project itself to disappear.[14] Building a new type of aircraft did not work in quite the same way as designing a drug. We are here in the domain of *applied research* of course. For the aim of the research programme, which began in the 1950s and was cancelled in 1965, was to design a militarily viable product, the TSR2, Britain's independent nuclear deterrent. Law argues that the very notion of 'the project' (2002: 87)[15] was not one thing but many, and we cannot, in his view, accept the rhetoric of such a 'project' being a 'communal' one. Its characteristics are better understood as multiplicity, fractionality and partiality.

It is interesting that his object of study is in fact an aircraft that, at the time, was acknowledged to be trying to combine too many different roles. It was an advanced weapons system, capable of all weather tactical strikes; it was a reconnaissance, remote-sensing, mapping and navigational system; it was a communications system; it was a fuel system (pipes, pumps, tanks and engines); it was global traveller in its reach – all depicted in a 1962 sales brochure through a series of separate drawings, diagrams and statements (2002: 13–15). What made the TSR2 impossible was the high level of performance demanded simultaneously of each component. The verdict, not long after its demise, was that it combined 'several roles in one aircraft, attempting to achieve compatibility in performance which had not previously been attempted', and its 'basic weakness [was] ... the attempt to meet too many new and complex specifications at the same time'; 'it proved intrinsically impossible to co-ordinate the airframe, electronics and engine work' (quotations from Williams, Gregory and Simpson 1969, in Law 2002: 33–4). Imagine, says Law (2002: 192), that there never was a single aircraft, there were several; what would be interesting would be to see how people went on talking as though there were one. At any rate, insofar as the operation worked, as it did for a while, it summoned a kind of 'fractional coherence', drawing things together without centring them, while endorsing the reticence of 'fractional knowing', and not making too much of a narrative out of things. Law dryly observes: 'the performance of technological agency is complex' (2002: 140).

One cannot read from off from a project, then, what kind of social community it will in turn generate, and certainly one cannot assume that it is a 'communal' one. In a decentred set of operations, such as described for the TSR2,[16] statements of common interest tell less than the whole story. 'The project' engages an array of people with an array of quite different interests, not all linked together, and individualised thereby .

So let us take a further step back, to the apparently elemental unit of the individual researcher: persons as knowledge-carriers. After all, and above all, knowledge travels with people.

3 The (researcher as a) person

We can talk of people as mobile when they move between communities; there are distinct circumstances when they are valued *because* they are at the same time carriers of knowledge. Whereas one of the preconditions for the mobility of the product is that knowledge is detachable from the person, here it moves precisely because it remains attached. Implicit or embodied knowledge goes wherever persons go (Harvey 1997). And included in this knowledge may be the very capacities that also make them, as persons, mobile: namely knowledge of networks. The 'knowledge-worker' prized by companies may be prized, among other things, for the connections they bring (Hill and Turpin 1995). Companies may in turn try to stop the dispersal of expertise by holding on to people through enhancing other aspects of their lives. This is the familiar phenomenon of engendering corporate loyalty.[17]

What we might infer about communities here is the possibility of people joining them or leaving them at will. The knowledge that is attached to them goes with individuals when they leave one job for another, moving locations; insofar as their knowledge was originally created in the company of others, then it is the community from which they take. It is visible in being left behind. But in what sense can a person ever leave a previous community (so to speak) completely behind (Beer 1989)? To the extent that knowledge is embedded in what they do, it will in turn show traces of their training, occupation and the contexts in which they have used it. Academics took note of the fact, for example, that the first generation of QAA personnel were drawn from schools inspectors, and it has been observed more than once that many of the anthropologists who were active as feminist scholars in the 1970s had in the 1990s extended their interests to issues in the new technologies.

But it would be a mistake to suppose that, even where people are both mobile and valued as carriers of knowledge, it is a *knowledge-community* which commands their first loyalty. The markers of mobility may be misleading. They need not point to contexts that the knowledge acquisition has created: persons can at the same time be inhabiting communities of quite different, extraneous, origin, and ones that give them the reasons for travel.

In a sense this is a totally banal statement: people can be knowledge-workers *and* switch jobs for reasons that have nothing to do with that. Other things may cause them to move. So let me touch on a rather different kind of mobility, where physical movement is perhaps reinforced on a humdrum, daily basis, or re-enacted that way as people move (so to speak) between reference points in their heads. My example comes from a research project, and – paradoxically perhaps – from the very effort that goes in attempts to embed individual persons in their immediate milieu by building up a *common ethos*.[18]

There could be no more committed knowledge-workers than those who investigate Artificial Life. At once more modest and more ambitious than Artifical Intelligence, this is a field dedicated to computer simulation and thus to synthesising knowledge, explicitly making new knowledge out of old. A deliberately fresh way of thinking about biology: a plan 'to capture on computers ... the formal properties of organisms, populations, and ecoystems' (Helmreich 1998b: 8), not to speak of the evolution of forms. The Sante Fe Institute for the Sciences of Complexity, founded in the 1980s, dedicated to multidisciplinary scientific research, became a focus for this kind of work. One of the things that bound the individual researchers to their work, and generated a particular sense of community, was the common language that they evolved among themselves.

Now that language did not reflect the remoteness and exclusivity that people may have felt about their location, but instead gestured towards life outside it; it was not only tied to the workplace, but jumped beyond. Into computer models of evolutionary process were transplanted ideas about genetics, reproduction and kinship (Helmreich 1998b: 208). 'Mating' (the mutual exchange of computer code) is usually accomplished through a 'genetic algorithm' – a computational procedure that can 'evolve' solutions to complex problems by generating populations of possible solutions, and by treating these solutions metaphorically as individuals that can 'mate', 'mutate' and 'compete' to 'survive and 'reproduce'. 'Two parents are selected according to fitness and material between them is exchanged to produced two children which replace them (Helmreich 2001: 129). I quote from an algorithmist: 'In nature, crossover occurs when two parents exchange parts of their corresponding chromosomes. In a genetic algorithm, crossover recombines the genetic material in two parent chromosomes to make two children' (Helmreich 2001: 129).[xix] Now, although it could be argued that the analogy with genetics and kinship is being used in a very generalised way, as indeed many biologists do, Helmreich also describes how the almost uniformly male researchers cast themselves into very explicit *paternal* roles. '[M]en are more frustrated in the urge to create life than women' (1998b: 215).

These people might seem remote in what they do, but not in the lives they lead – they *borrow* a social discourse from elsewhere (kinship and paternity): for some of them from home, for all of them from a wider society in which they are embedded. So, instead of finding a community that exaggerates exclusiveness, we find at its heart an alien discourse, an unexpected immigrant. Knowledge is cast in metaphors which serve to bulwark common values, but come themselves from a quite different quarter.[20] So persons ferry knowledge about, drawing on different aspects of their own biographies, in ways that may be quite unpredictable.

The purpose of this narrative has been to see what the carriers tell us about the communities they form. With knowledge travelling in the form of products, between participants in a project, and embodied in persons, we have traversed three salient junctions in the process of knowledge production: individual workers, their joint enterprise and their output. Different sorts of communities have winked in and out of prominence, leaving perhaps a sense of scepticism about how much one can infer. At the end of this particular, and rather short, road we came across a bunch of knowledge-producers who have themselves jumped ship – as persons leading the multiple lives all persons do, they introduced a quite different set of issues to talk about their common values. They prompt me to change direction. A new question: what happens when people become *aware of* (or bring into focus) the fact that knowledge is embedded in persons?

Consumption: Creating Circuits of Communication

What creates a community need not be commonality of interest or of purpose in production, but can just as well be practices of consumption. The developers of enabling technologies frequently appeal to 'community' benefits. Here the term is mobilised not just for the purposes of description, but as a self-description which is also a term for action, a call to arms.[21] Community becomes a goal;[22] and identifying a community in contexts where practices of communication create recognisable purposes and intelligible values becomes a target.[23] Communication is a good, in and of itself, inherently desirable.[24] It is as though my question of how knowledge is made portable is turned into the participants' question of *how to make* knowledge portable. Here are a couple of instances.

1 Planned circuits

My examples are of *communities based on technology*. Or rather, the planning thereof; the first was locked for ever in the future (Cleal 2001).[25]

The inhabitants of several of the islands found off the coast of Denmark were in the late 1990s selected as 'a model target and end user example' for the European Network for Intelligent Information Interfaces.[26] Unlike the aircraft, for example, and more akin perhaps to the artificial life experimentation, the project was not task-oriented; there was no specific activity around which users and designers could collaborate. More open-ended than that, it sought ways of integrating common and already existing communication technologies in order to facilitate interaction among people otherwise remote from one another. The idea was to create a communications circuit, particular to these people's circumstances, that would function as a collaborative working environment, and it was called 'The Magic Lounge' (ML).[27] If people can communicate easily they can also learn from one another: open up contacts, get into touch in unexpected ways with others not normally forming part of their circle, save the hours of travel it takes to get to meetings. The emphasis was on what the technology could facilitate and what, above all, must be facilitated is communication.

Before all that, however, what had to be communicated (to the designers) was what the users wanted. The Intelligent Information Interfaces (i3) programme was driven by the notion of 'participatory design'.[28] One problem was how to engage the Danish islanders without being able to present the islanders with a working example – on their screens or down their telephone lines – of what the designers had in mind, because it had not yet been made. The ideal, though, was clear:

> Participatory design ... often takes user needs as they are described by the users themselves, and in doing so disregards the potential for innovative human practices (not easily fore-seeable by the users) embedded in technological innovation. Therefore, software developers, when aiming to invent innovative systems, seem to be forced to disregard the users and to develop technological innovations per se ... [T]his weakness can be avoided ... [by focusing on] the design of *innovative interaction patterns* and not in the development of innovative technologies. (Agostini, De Michelis and Susani 1998: 5; my emphasis)[29]

In short, what was needed was the formation of an innovative community to live up to, so to speak, the potential of the technology.

Whereas saving people from isolation by putting them in touch may be an end in itself,[30] leading to a circulation of knowledge in a weak sense (getting to know about other people), effecting the circulation of knowledge may also be done in a strong sense, with the intention to equip persons with usable information.[31] Enabling people to tap into new circuits of communication can be truly didactic, meeting the late twentieth- and early twenty-first-century demand for informed citizens or, in Putkonen's (2001) words, 'global subjects'.[32] In the information society, with its commitment to evidence-based policy, ensuring that knowledge travels begins to carry political and moral burdens.

Another experiment was going on about the same time in Manchester. But Manchester's plan to become an 'Infocity' was able to draw on existing facilities to move rapidly – more rapidly than the Magic Lounge people could – into a situation where users had a medium to work with. The Infocity was a consortium of civic ventures that coalesced in 1997–8 in order to take the possibilities for teleconnections to a higher level than ever before. The already established Greater Manchester Information Network Group (G-MING)[33] now installed high-speed connections between computers in several institutions, while the Manchester Communities Information Network (MCIN),[34] equally well established, set up public access kiosks throughout the city (Agar, Green and Harvey 2002).[35] The aim was to tackle an old community problem (the decline of post-industrial cities) by envisaging a new foundation to community life (exploiting unprecedented possibilities for connections).

Among the institutional users of the technical service was the Museum of Science and Industry in Manchester. Its staff, educators to the core, saw themselves as enhancing the kind of information they could disseminate. Here we can almost talk of *planned knowledge communities*. Almost: the synapses did not fire quite as expected. The reason sounds a little familiar.

> The Museum staff's interest was in the 'communicative' potentials of these technologies; their understanding of a network was of a linkage of persons and machine, of distributed responsibilities and dynamic outcomes. G-MING's interest was in providing the hardware for other people to do things with; what other people did was largely up to them. (Agar, Green and Harvey 2002: 280)

As the authors comment, there were two quite different understandings of network in operation. G-MING provided an infrastructure that did not interfere with people's liberty to consume it as they liked, while the Museum staff saw persons and machines linked together in a joint creative process, 'in mutually constitutive relationships of possibility, in which science and politics are thoroughly entangled, and in which agency depends on exchanges of information and expertise' (Agar, Green and Harvey 2002: 280). They thus saw themselves as creative consumers, expecting to be part of the programme design, and assumed they would be involved in discussions; instead, as participants in the i3 knew could happen all too easily, even under the rubric of participatory design, they were locked out of the technological community, to be brought in as 'users' at the end.

2 Policy vectors

The need to ensure wide access, knowledge convergence if you like, can actually create *divergent communities* in its wake. I am thinking of knowledge disseminated in a directed and therefore partial (partisan) way. This is specific-purpose as opposed to general-purpose dissemination, intentionally partial in that it is aimed at persons who simply need this one bit of knowledge to inform them about some action or decision (e.g. what the benefits of taking the drug Taxol would be).[36] This can in turn create the need for regulation by government as a protective device: because people are getting part-knowledge, they cannot assess the whole of it. Insofar as the knowledge creates persons only knowledgeable in parts, it may presume part-communities or no communities at all.

The Manchester example prompts us into thinking about the divergence between carriers of expert and local (the public, the laity) opinion, a distinction defined by differential access to the knowledge in question. 'Public Understanding of Science' programmes of the 1970s–90s pointed to just such divergence. But the late twentieth and early twenty-first centuries have witnessed a new move: the explicit recognition that consumers need to be brought into the production process itself ('Public Engagement with Science'). In so far as producers and consumers in the fields of science and its publics form communities, it is claimed, they need to be merged as *co-participants*.[37] I refer to the call to arms from Nowotny and her colleagues (Gibbons *et al.* 1994; Nowotny *et al.* 2001, and see Endnote to this collection). They argue that science has become increasingly entangled with its social context, for that context has started (in their memorable phrase) 'speaking back', turning from background into agent. Science and society cease to operate as separate domains (they 'co-mingle'), while each retains enough gravitational pull to have distinct trajectories described as 'co-evolutionary'. The political intention of these authors, to put it too briefly, is to have us appreciate the open-endedness and context-sensitive nature of contemporary science as strengths rather than weaknesses. It is a powerful thing to say, that all the interventions and disseminations that enlarge the application of science in fact point to where we want it to go: towards a 'socially robust' science.

The point was translated into action by the *Quincennial Review of the Research Councils* in 2001 (Office of Science and Technology) which laid the foundation for Research Councils UK. It addresses the Research Councils together. A principal concern is with delivery, that is, with how research funded by the government should be seen to have an impact. What is needed is a 'clearer strategic framework for delivering science', and for applying 'principles of public service delivery ... [in] dealings with users' (DTI 2001: 1–2). Principles of public service delivery were written into the way the report itself was produced, such as '[to] consult and involve' (DTI 2001: 11), which included open consultation by the OST website.[38] Now 'stakeholders' and 'users' are roles; people in these roles may or may not form communities of their own. But the driving notion is that if they can be brought into the scientific process, they will have become part of a wider social entity. The *Review*'s metaphor has a familiar ring in Cambridge: among its strategic goals is joining up with stakeholders so as to work with them in a more collegiate fashion. Of course this collegiality will only work if, in turn, knowledge has managed to travel – if knowledge reaches the stakeholders and they can in turn export their own knowledge to influence the publicising of scientific developments.

An Experiment in Knowledge or an Experiment in Community?

I have distributed these comments across a number of locations, seemingly at will, with no organic connection between them. Incidentally and expediently, the dispersal comes from the nature of secondary sources: no one account tells you all you desire to know. That desire in turn seems limitless. So wandering across an open campus, this might have been no more than a Frazerian journey, an undisciplined plucking of exemplars from the roadside. And so it might, but for one thing. And that is the real life experiment on the doorstep. Not limitless at all.

The CGKP is conceived of as a coherent, and in that sense, single entity, though by definition it embraces multiple possibilities under its umbrella. It is a real-life organisation of many, complex, different kinds of knowledge, and I would surprised if there were not elements of all – and more – of the situations I have described within its net. In a weak sense, each case has involved an attempt by people to organise themselves in relation to what they acknowledge as complex interactions, and, whether or not they succeed, there is something valuable to be learnt from them. In a much stronger sense, I imagine that within the purview of the CGKP I could find examples to replicate all the various modes of travel I have been talking about. Certainly it is dedicated to making knowledge mobile in both senses of the term, at once portable and creating the circuits of transport. But what about the kinds of communities one could infer?

You will recall those terms cited at the outset: departments, research centres, laboratories, partners... They all point to social configurations, but none tells you the nature of their sociality. One small way in – a way towards thinking about the nature of their sociality – might be to think about the kinds of communities created in the wake of knowledge as it travels in its diverse directions.

NOTES

Acknowledgement: The theme of this paper comes from one of Ian Donaldson's rubrics for a CRASSH conference (see end): 'How is innovative knowledge transmitted from one kind of community to another... What happens to such knowledge as it travels.'

Bryan Cleal and Ingrid Putkonen have both kindly allowed me to draw on unpublished work. I am grateful to Alison Stewart, not just for chairing the original talk but for her questions afterwards. I also very much appreciate the comments of the Anthropology Department at Goldsmiths, London, who heard this as a seminar paper, as well as subsequent observations from Eric Hirsch.

1 Taken (in each case) from the *Proposal to the Department of Health and DTI*, 2001, initiated by the Public Health Genetics Unit, with thanks to Dr R. Zimmern. Knowledge Parks originate in the need articulated by the Department of Health to support research in human genetics and its application to medicine by bringing together multiple aspects of emerging developments and by trying to ensure their acceptability to the public. Of several bids (of which six were successful), the Cambridge proposal goes furthest in responding to the tender invitation to develop appropriate economic, ethical, legal and social frameworks for the effective delivery of genetic services.

2 Later, an *advisory panel*, as well as *associates*, joined them (http://www.cgkp.org.uk).

3 Knowledge is only useful, it is claimed, if others can have access to it. The CGKP will concentrate its efforts at dissemination and education on three groups: (a) health *professionals* (b) *policy makers* (c) *scientists/entrepreneurs* and *commercial partners* (Zimmern 2001). (Italics mine, to continue the listing above.)

4 The challenge that Ian Donaldson, Director of CRASSH, threw down for the Conference (see acknowledgement). It is answered in one vein by proponents of Actor Network Theory: Mol and Law 1994 remains for me the classic travelogue.

5 Not a term I have ever been happy with as an analytic. I use it throughout 'ethnographically', that is, assuming nothing more than its common usage implies.

6 I deliberately leave aside knowledge communities found within formal structures of association generated by companies and business firms, or by departments and faculties, or by disciplines and arenas of expertise, which presuppose common interests, common 'cultures' of operation. This is not to say that they are not interesting, but arenas self-conscious about 'mixing' expertises sharpen certain salient issues.

7 Of course, borrowings do not have to entail transactions. One of the few anthropological accounts of traffic between disciplines is Schlecker and Hirsch (2001). This is a study of the way the fields of media and cultural studies, and science technology studies, took up the concept of 'ethnography'. Anthropology has taken many things back for its own usage. The result is a kind of implicit or embedded interdisciplinarity that requires no tokens of agreement or disagreement.

8 Bronwyn Parry's work on the transformation of substances into information has several remarkable insights important here (forthcoming). At each point at which knowledge about its properties migrated from one product to another (from the bark to the extract to the molecular formula to the chemical compound), different communities of experts (botanists, chemists, pharmaceutical researchers, companies) were involved.

9 Scientific findings build upon one another, and 'scientists buttress their new claims by connecting them as much as possible to the body of previous scientific literature' (Biagioli 2000: 88). He refers to the 'community-specific' nature of scientific authorship.

10 Gusterson (2003: 301) describes scientists as despising the academic culture, with its focus on publications and citations.

11 Thanks to Ludek Broz for emphasizing this point. Commissions of enquiry and ethics committees afford other examples.

12 This does not begin to describe the social realities, see for example Barry 2001, ch. 7.

13 Huge US Government investment in exploiting the yew bark, over the course of some 30 years, was a 'failure' until events took an unexpected turn with the pharmaceutical company.

14 The programme was scrapped as part of a new policy measure by an incoming government, but among the reasons it was scrapped were problems with delivery.

15 This multiplicity was effaced, and the enterprise could be *performed* as though it encapsulated a common goal.

16 He would intend us to understand many operations as exactly so, the aircraft project – deploying tens of thousands of people – being just an example.

17 See below: a kind of intended community.

18 An exemplary study here is Georgina Born (1995) on the avant garde experimental music centre IRCAM.

19 I quote the deliberate use of analogy here because of its clear role in knowledge-making (not all metaphors or analogies work this way).

20 These are 'merographic relations': this is a model, for the way in which anything that comes into focus is also part of something else (Strathern 1992).

21 I thank Mark Henare for this prompt.

22 A well known move from the implicit to explicit (Strathern 1992), and a long established proclivity (e.g. newcomers to a village wanting to see it activated as 'a village' or the QAA that wants a university to be seen to be 'a university'), documented most recently by Miller 2003.

23 As though Luhmann's (1990: chap 1) model for sociality (society as a network of communication) were being animated.

24 On the self-defining virtues of connections, see Green and Harvey 1999 (and I am grateful for permission to cite this); also Wittel, Lury and Lash 2002 on interactivity and technological citizenship, Barry 2001: chap 6.

25 And was never in the end fully realised.

26 From Andersen 1998. I am grateful to Bryan Cleal for the copy of the ENiii in-house magazine (*i3 Magazine*), for all other information included in this section, and for permission to quote from his unpublished dissertation (2001).

27 People will already have social interests, drawn from their own circumstances; these do not have to be integrated because each person can instead be integrated into a wider circuit which makes available what he or she wants.

28 From Agostini, De Michelis and Susani 1998; while it drew from another part of the i3 programme, the ethos would have been recognisable to the Magic Lounge project.

29 The authors begin their piece saying: 'The design of computer based systems willing to support social interaction among users is not a technological problem' (i.e. it is a social one).

30 At one point it would seem the ML designers imagined that they would be creating a community of locals who would enhance their own community initiatives through being in easier contact with one another than they had been. However, the potential users saw little point in further developing local contacts: they saw the facility as giving them access to those not on

the islands, to the world outside. (One might see this as another version of the Santa Fe incorporation of 'extraneous' reference points.)

31 In the Danish case, for example, distance learning for children, more effective advertising to tourists, and, in general, practical work tools rather than recreational opportunities.

32 Where, among other things, people have to learn how to communicate with themselves.

33 It built on an earlier venture, regarded as 'revolutionary' at the time, a publicly owned file server involving several organisations in the city. The original G-MING network was funded under the EU's 4th Framework. Infocities, a further European initiative, with seven of them across the continent, were a sub-group of over 50 Telecities (of which Manchester was one), with an agenda based on the idea of harnessing telematics not only to make cities more attractive places to live, but to get people to *use* cities in 'more flexible ways' (Agar, Green and Harvey 2002: 277).

34 The long-standing aim of the MCIN was to bring together 'community information' from diverse places and make it widely available.

35 Being well established also meant these operations had their own agendas. I have, of course, abbreviated the account here, and this is not the place to go into the complicated relations between the two (which led, at one point, to 'serious rupture' (Agar, Green and Harvey 2002: 283)).

36 The Canadian Royal Commisson on New Reproductive Technologies (see Endnote), and its advocacy of evidence-based policy, equipped the public it was consulting with the information they needed to make opinions.

37 Or we may find communities in alliance with one another. Responsibilities of the researcher extend into the design and delivery of products (see Nuffield Council 2002). What this means is that how knowledge gets carried beyond the producers and authors feeds back into the institutional underpinnings of the original process.

38 The following admonition to address the science and society agenda through 'consultation, engagement and dialogue' carries the warning that this must not be a passive matter of dissemination: 'the views of the concerned public should be actively sought' (DTI 2001: 61).

REFERENCES

Agar, J., Green, S. and Harvey, P. 2002 'Cotton to computers: From industrial to information revolutions', in S. Woolgar (ed.) *Virtual Society? Technology, Cyberbole, Reality,* Oxford: Oxford University Press.

Agostini, A., De Michelis, G. and Susani, M. 1998 'A methodology for the design of innovative user oriented systems', *i3 Magazine* 2: 4–7.

Andersen, L. N. 1998 'Magic Lounge in Saarbrücken', *i3 Magazine* 2: 10–11.

Barry, A. 2001 *Political Machines: Governing a Technological Society,* London: Athlone Press.

Beer, G. 1989 'Can the native return?', Hilda Hume Memorial Lecture, University of London.

Biagioli, M. 2000 'Right or rewards? Changing contexts and definitions of scientific authorship', *Journal of College and University Law* 27: 83–108.

Biagioli, M. and Galison, P. 2003 *Scientific Authorship: Credit and Intellectual Property in Science*, New York: Routledge.

Born, G. 1995 *Rationalizing Culture: IRCAM, Boulez and the Institutionalisation of the Musical Avant-garde*, Berkeley & Los Angeles: University of California Press.

Cleal, B. 2001 'Capturing community: innovation and technology within a European framework', doctoral dissertation, Dept. Social Anthropology, Cambridge.

DTI (Department of Trade and Industry) 2001 *Quinquennial Review of the Grant-awarding Research Councils,* London: Office of Science and Technology.

Gibbons, M., Limoges, C., Nowotny, H., Schwartzman, S., Scott, P., and Trow, M. 1994 *The New Production of Knowledge: The Dynamics of Science and Research in Contemporary Society,* London: Sage Publications.

Gibbons, M. 1999 'Science's new social contract with society', *Nature* 402 (Supp.) C81–4.

Goodman, J. and Walsh, V. 2001 *The Story of Taxol: Nature and Politics in the Pursuit of an Anti-cancer Drug,* Cambridge: Cambridge University Press.

Green, S. and Harvey, P. 1999 'Scaling places and networks: An ethnography of ICT "innovation" in Manchester', presented at Internet and Ethnography Conference, Hull.

Gusterson, H. 2003 'The death of the authors of death: Prestige and creativity among nuclear weapons scientists', in M. Biagioli and P. Galison (eds), *Scientific Authorship: Credit and Intellectual Property in Science*, New York: Routledge.

Harvey, P. (ed.) 1997 *Technology as Skilled Practice* (special issue), *Social Analysis* 41(1).

Helmreich, S. 1998a *Silicon Second Nature: Culturing Artificial Life in a Digital World,* Berkeley: University of California Press.

—— 1998b 'Replicating reproduction in artificial life: or, the essence of life in the age of virtual electronic reproduction', in S. Franklin and H. Ragoné (eds), *Reproducing Reproduction: Kinship, Power, and Technological Innovation,* Philadelphia: University of Pennsylvania Press.

—— 2001 'Kinship in hypertext: transubstantiating fatherhood and informational flow in artificial life', in S. Franklin and S. McKinnon (eds) *Relative Values: Reconfiguring Kinship Studies,* Durham, NC: Duke University Press.

Hill, S. and Turpin, T. 1995 'Cultures in collision: The emergence of new localism in academic research', in M. Strathern (ed.), *Shifting Contexts; Transformations in Anthropological Knowledge,* London: Routledge.

Law, John 2002 *Aircraft Stories: Decentering the Object in Technoscience*, Durham, NC: Duke University Press

Luhmann, N. 1990 *Essays on Self-reference*, New York: Columbia University Press.

Miller, D. 2003 'The virtual moment', *JRAI* (ns) 9: 57–75.

Mol, A. and Law, J. 1994 'Regions, networks and fluids: Anaemia and social typology', *Social Studies of Science* 24: 641–71.

Nowotny, H., Scott, P. and Gibbons, M. 2001 *Re-Thinking Science: Knowledge and the Public in an Age of Uncertainty*, Oxford: Polity.

Nuffield Council 2002 *The Ethics of Research Related to Healthcare in Developing Countries*, London: Nuffield Council on Bioethics.

Parry, B.C. [forthcoming] *The Fate of the Collections: Revealing the Social and Spatial Dynamics of Global Trade in 'Bio-Commodities'*, New York: Columbia University Press

Putkonen, I. 2001 'The global subject: a study of a family planning NGO, globalisation and the shaping of subjectivity', doctoral dissertation, Dept. Social Anthropology, Cambridge.

Schlecker, M. and Hirsch, E. 2001 'Incomplete knowledge: ethnography and the crisis of context in studies of media, science and technology', *History of the Human Sciences* 14: 69–87.

Schön, Donald A. 1991 [1983] *The Reflective Practitioner: How Professionals Think in Action*, Aldershot: Ashgate Publishing Ltd.

Strathern, M. 1992 *After Nature: English Kinship in the Late Twentieth Century*, Cambridge: Cambridge University Press.

Wittel, A., Lutz, C. and Lash, S. 2002 'Real and virtual connectivity: New media in London', in S. Woolgar (ed.) *Virtual Society? Technology, Cyberbole, Reality*, Oxford: Oxford University Press.

Zimmern, R. 2001 The Cambridge Genetics Knowledge Park: A Proposal for the Department of Health and the Department of Trade and Industry (pers. comm.).

From: 'The Organization of Knowledge', CRASSH Conference, Cambridge, April 2003. Session: 'Knowledge communities', convenor Prof. Martin Daunton.

WORKING PAPER TWO
Commons and Borderlands

The argument of this Working Paper is plucked directly from Beer's work, and the questions she asks of interdisciplinarity in the context of nineteenth-century science. They prompt the thought that the way we make extra training explicit to ourselves separates a self-conscious interdisciplinarity off from the routine and everyday ability to mix knowledges. But science also throws up some interesting issues of ownership. Here a social scientist reflects on the double need for clearly defined authors and for collaborators, interpreters and allies.

> Ideas cannot survive long lodged within a single domain. They need the traffic of the apparently *in*appropriate audience.
> (Gillian Beer, *Open Fields*, 1996)

The nub of my argument is plucked directly from Gillian Beer's work. She poses a series of questions at the heart of the exercise in which we are engaged, namely 'interdisciplinarity'.

> How thoroughly interdisciplinary is it possible to be? Are we lightly transferring a set of terms from one practice to another, as metaphor, *façon de parler*? Are we appropriating *materials* hitherto neglected for analysis of the kind we have always used? Or are we trying to learn new *methods* and skills fast, which other have spent years acquiring? (1996: 115, orig. emphasis.)

If we work solely within the terms established by our initial training, she goes on to observe, 'we may find ourselves caught in a monstrous self-referentiality' (1996: 116). It is the way we make extra training explicit to ourselves which separates a self-conscious interdisciplinarity off from the routine and everyday ability to mix knowledges.

Her questions are posed of nineteenth-century science. And contained within them are, I think, her own earlier insights into certain nineteenth-century dilemmas. I see etched against her three questions, several others; they spring from concerns with the nature of perceived similarities. These are expressed, for instance, in the preoccupations of Darwin and his peers about single or multiple origins, about whether one is talking of humankind or indeed of all kinds. And the problem that appears to inhere in the data (the demonstration of a single line of descent) becomes transposed to the method. When writers use the language of kinship, say, to draw attention to affinities and similarities, is the connection one of analogy and metaphor (that is, how language is being used) or is the connection a genetic one (that is, a demonstrable kinship between phenomena)? Where does the creative energy lie? In the study of language itself, the contrast collapses when resemblances between languages are taken to indicate to connections between them (1996: 107).

Of disciplines too one might ask, are the crossovers a matter of analogy or do they index genetic connections? That is, does one discipline open up imaginative possibilities for expression, providing mutual metaphors, as Beer describes for evolutionary theory and language; or is there a cross-fertilisation that transforms methods and objects of enquiry, as anthropologists who once talked of 'the literary turn' in their subject were claiming? In other words, what kind of creativity is at issue here?

Now it would be a mistake to think that the genetic kinship was the profounder intellectual connection. When in 1888 Francis Galton, then President of the Royal Anthropological Institute, heard Tylor's paper comparing marriage and kinship across some 350 societies, he was concerned about the prior historical connections that might lie unknown between them. Analogical relations would have been much cleaner. For where cases were independent units, one could compare analogous developments, but where there were pre-existing links, units lost their singular identities and comparison lost its statistical rigour. This became known as 'Galton's problem': the non-independence of sampling units.[1] One might add that where systems appear analogous and comparison becomes possible, the possibilities bifurcate again: between the substantive comparisons that elucidate the effects of similar and dissimilar practices in different contexts, and the metaphorical illuminations that come from using concepts derived from the *study* of one ethnographic arena to deploy in another.

Literary questions can also be anthropological ones, then. The enquiry about the analogic or genetic origins of constructs – about figurative or literal connections – are of intense interest to the anthropologist's comparative method. But I want to draw Gillian Beer's thoughts along in another direction, and I begin with kinship metaphors.

Single Origins, Single Outcomes

The evolutionists' search for affinity put common origins back in time. They were looking for common ancestry, for an undivided past.[2] Of course that notion of ancestry was already pared down to the singularity of a lineal connection (Beer 1983). Indeed, the evolutionist would be satisfied to find one distant progenitor, 'the common parent' (two would spoil the genealogy – the problem is neatly solved by ideas about non-interbreeding, self-reproducing species, which gives you two parents of one kind). Interdisciplinarists, on the other hand, might well reintroduce the notion of marriage into affinity: their hope rests in the common offspring, the child of different parents, who will take after both sides, sides that before may have been as unlike to one another as species are. For interdisciplinarity is premised on the subsequent merging of what once had distinct origins, and looks, so to speak, to an undivided future.

There is a very contemporary interest in this. As the late twentieth-century to early twenty-first-century research university moves out of its earlier and deliberately constructed isolation – isolation from the public in general and from commerce in particular – two pressures appear at odds with one another. And it is helpful to think through these pressures with the aid of the procreative analogies Beer calls to mind. Both concern knowledge and the public good. The difference is between the search for undivided outcomes and the search for undivided origins.

Undivided outcomes

What was once the obvious brachiation of scholarly routes to knowledge has become, at turn of the century, familiar rhetoric in Higher Education: an explicit value is accorded interdisciplinary activity. Unity of outcome does not require a homogeneous and undifferentiated object; rather, it consists in an object held in common, the joint product, multi-authored, of diverse efforts. The mobilisation of energy that often follows is impressive. The trick is to prevent the promise of such energy from becoming a new form of monstrous self-referentiality (I take the phrase from Beer) – where interdisciplinarity is no longer the corrective to too much in-looking, but itself becomes an idea that constantly plays back on itself; becomes its own end, a jacked- up explicitness to meet new demands for funding and accountability regimes in Higher Education. Fixing interdisciplinarity into institutions means that simple analogic exhaustion (Beer 1996: 110) won't prise the separate elements apart again. But there is a countervailing pressure, of equal explosiveness, in the late twentieth century/early twenty-first century, which might. This is the pressure to seek origins of a particular kind.

Undivided origins

I am thinking of the renewed onus on universities to treat investment seriously in the context of a debate that has gone suitably public.[3] Against the experience of the shared input that collaborators and scholars have in one another's enterprises, specifying the origin of a work alters the terrain. When ownership comes into the picture, it need not matter however many origins there are if each can be distinctly and uniquely claimed – there are so to speak simply several 'ones'.[4] This is true whether the issue is directly that of intellectual property or not. IPR includes patents, which search out the identity of an inventor or, equally, the identity of the source of the funding; and copyright, which records the originator of a form of expression, regardless of how profound or original in that sense the expression is (Barron 1998). Questions of owning also affect scientific authorship, which lies largely outside the realm of IPR as such, where claims to forms of expression are trivial or irrelevant beside the importance of claiming a usable idea or validating the sources of information

(Biagioli and Galison 2003). The point is that collaboration can be unpicked to identify the individual person, or the individual team, with whom the origin rests undivided. Disciplinary identity could well be re-born at such moments.

These two pressures are among the changes that have already altered the university landscape that had carried most of us through most of the twentieth century. With Gillian Beer as a guide, I want to go back to the period towards the end of the nineteenth century, when that landscape was being put in place.

Complexities from the Start

There are many strands one could pursue. The rubric 'Open Fields' (see end) invites one to muse on the notion of commons, on images of freely available circulation of knowledge for all, notwithstanding the fact that there is never any terra nullus, that inventions are always in part re-inventions, and thus always someone else's as well. Yet they may require novel forms of expression. Discovery and inventions (in the sense of fiction) are uneasy allies, in writing as much as in claiming property in inventions (as in manufacture) that leaves discovery in the public domain. But I wish instead to write about borderlands.

The kind of 'conscious appropriation and re-appropriation' that Beer (1996: 95) notes between Darwinian evolutionary theory and language theory in the nineteenth century is repeated over and over again. I point to an arena of interdisciplinary fervour that has a very contemporary ring to it. Yet a concurrent desire for autonomy involved, to the contrary, repudiating and suppressing links between fields. Of disciplines, she says, '[I]t also seems that for theory to conceive itself as authentic and to establish itself as free-standing, it needs to obliterate traces of dependence and to repudiate analogies with other forms of learning' (1996: 95). Here I sketch in some of the background to this desire as it appeared in property law. In the process I transpose the argument from disciplines to authors, in order to open up possible connections – analogic, genetic – between them. We shall return to origins and outcomes at the end.

It is James Clerk Maxwell's electromagnetic kinds of waves that Beer's own title brings partly in mind. She puts him the company of the anxious scientists of the time who had to find, through the artifice of language, a mode of communicating the new realisms. This, she diagnoses (1996: 197), is modernism indeed. 'Among Victorian scientists we uncover anxieties about the relativity of knowledge, about determinism, about imagining a stochastic universe instead of a teleological one, about manifestation, symbol, and discourse.' She goes on to suggest that Maxwell himself was highly conscious of the changing functions of metaphor 'as they extend across scientific fields' (1996: 309).[5] But what helped exposition did not necessarily help comprehension.

A historian of science has recently taken up the issue in an interesting way. Andrew Warwick interrogates the authorship of the classic 1873 *Treatise on Electricity and Magnetism,* originally intended as an advanced textbook to accompany Maxwell's new teaching duties. Beer stresses the highly disciplined way in which Maxwell tried to deal with language, avoiding taking refuge in popular expository rhetoric.[6] 'Even his puns are models of precision' (Beer 1996: 310). Warwick takes the precision further: authorship divides, and divides the writer into different persons, each with their own canons of precision.[7]

There is an initial contrast between the preface in which (with a constant stress on the first person) 'Maxwell asserts that it is *his* accomplishment to have mathematized Michael Faraday's electromagnetic theory', and the tenor of the general body of the text, where 'the demonstration of technical proofs and theorems becomes [in the use of the inclusive 'we'] the joint accomplishment of author and reader' (Warwick 2003: 134–5, original emphasis). Yet, whereas the preface is totally comprehensible, the text is not. The narrative makes assumptions far beyond any one reader's competence. 'Suddenly', says Warwick, 'the reader is confronted by specialized vocabularies and turns of phrase from electrical engineering, electrical theory, metrology, and higher mathematics' (2003: 135). Part of the complication lies in the number of authorial selves here. They come from several disciplines.[8]

> What is ... unusual about the authorial selves presented in the Treatise is the way in which he [Maxwell] speaks sometimes as a physical theorist, sometimes as a mathematician, and some-times as an electrical engineer. ... [And] those who hoped to find

something akin to his overall understanding ... needed to possess at least a comparable range of skills. (2003: 136)

No one did, but some possessed some of them, and Warwick describes the struggles of Cambridge mathematicians to understand the book and teach it to undergraduates. They found it frankly hard going – not just the novel physical theory or experimental electricity, but the idiosyncratic way in which he applied mathematics often proved 'impenetrable'.[9] Maxwell's own lectures were not of much use, and it was left to college lecturers to try to turn the *Treatise* into a real textbook. We know the most notable of these people. With the supervisor ('coach') Edward Routh[10] setting himself the task of mastering the sections he thought most relevant to undergraduates, and William Niven's intercollegiate classes at Trinity College, the Cambridge mathematicians became convinced of the work's importance. The result was a 'collective activity' which enabled them 'to pool their skills in puzzling out opaque passages and difficult derivations', and to discriminate with confidence between problems requiring interpretation, errors, and unfinished thinking (2003: 151).[11] Warwick concludes:

> What enabled much of Maxwell's project in electromagnetism to be reconstructed so effectively in Cambridge in the 1870s was the distributed presence of very similar selves among the coaches, intercollegiate lecturers, and, in time, demonstrators at the Cavendish Laboratory. (2003: 153)

Those similar selves related of course to only some of Maxwell's several disciplinary trajectories; having to be explained, his work is re-authored. At the same time those distributed selves occupied fields of overlapping if not identical interests, and could thus regard one another as having an output in common.

All that remains to be said is that the story neither finishes there, nor with Maxwell's death in 1879. 'The rapid development of electromagnetic field theory through the 1880s, and, especially, the production of electromagnetic waves in 1888, prompted the Clarendon Press to commission a third edition of Maxwell's ... work' (2003: 155). J.J. Thompson famously took up the challenge, adding a large number of explanatory footnotes, and (in Warwick's words) generally accelerating the reader's journey through the book. It was no longer the cutting edge of electrical theory, but a textbook from which students should be learning the principles of science.

Accelerating the reader's journey was the rationale behind many volumes of the time that sought to render great works accessible. As the lawyer Corynne McSherry (2001) describes, one that was to gain significance far beyond the author's intention was *Aids to the study of moral philosophy*, put out in the early 1880s by an enterprising Glaswegian bookseller, William Sime. These were based on the notes a student had made of a series of lectures in philosophy given by a Professor Caird. The author, William Brown, argued in his preface that moral philosophy entails so much reading that 'no student, if left to himself, can undertake it successfully' (2001: 117), hence the aid. Presumably the notes were further reductions of what the university teacher had already reduced for his student audience. Caird himself was later to observe that the notes had been so badly taken that any association with them would damage his reputation. As we shall see, however, this was not to disavow authorship of the original but to assert it.[12]

If we think of all those similar and distributed selves in Cambridge who were the scientists, the lecturers, the supervisors and the students, and their concerns in common, they formed a collaborative network of sorts. Forced by the too-heterogeneous nature of Maxwell's interdisciplinary enterprise, they worked through a different kind of heterogeneity – a social constellation of different needs and expertise. The needs of students here were paramount. J.J. Thompson was a student who attended Niven's explanatory lectures (Warwick 2003: 150) before he became the editor of the third edition. But in other contexts barriers went up: social heterogeneity appeared not as a creative mix of skills and expectations, but as a bar to unregulated flow. Thus the pursuit of intelligibility could not, as events turned out, justify the fact that the Glasgow student had not sought permission for reproducing the philosopher's lectures. In 1887 the House of Lords, no less, ruled that students could not assume they were – in today's language that is – 'active participants in the reproduction of knowledge' (McSherry 2001: 121).

I will not dwell on the details of the case, but simply note that the arguments over authorship turned on the extent to which a lecturer was working in a public domain. What had happened was that, on discovering the volume, Professor Caird had sued for infringement of common law copyright. The bookseller appealed, and the decision went in his favour, on the grounds that a professor was a public official and his lectures were already in the public domain. The university existed for the diffusion of knowledge, and that knowledge was not to be confined to students. Caird went to the House of Lords and the Privy Council, who debated two questions: did a teacher in a public university own his lectures, and was giving a lecture a publication to the world? Only one voice was raised in favour of the bookseller's position, observing that it was a matter of public good that university teaching 'should be exposed to comment, to searching criticism and the full blaze of public opinion'. More than that, a professor's lectures were likened to a *gift* from the university or the professor to the nation. 'There was something unseemly in asserting individual rights where national interests were at stake' (McSherry 2001: 120).

The majority response, however, went against the bookseller. Caird was determined to be the creator of the work, 'a self-authorizing *magister* rather than a *rhetor* whose argument might be responsive to and shaped by an audience' (2001: 121).[13] Lecturing was an autonomous, one-way activity, and a study aid was a copy of the original. Moreover, students were not the general public, but a specialised group, and the professor a private individual speaking to other private individuals on the basis of an implicit contract regarding teaching and learning.[14] There was more here than a statement about authorship; this was part of the shaping of the new research university, whose usefulness to the nation, embodied in the state, lay precisely in its autonomy and distance from it. It served the nation not through engaging with the public, but through honing its expertise, exercising a monopoly of competence against the incursion of amateurs (2001: 123–4).[15]

From all this, 'authorship' emerges as what McSherry calls a 'boundary object'.[16] That is, it may be invoked in different ways. She herself is interested in contemporary debates between the market position, which portrays academic and, especially, scientific knowledge as liable to commercial exploitation, and the standpoint which portrays the academic community as an arena where the circulation of knowledge can be likened to the circulation of gifts, and the rewards of authorship as those of prestige or – in the case of science (e.g. Biagioli 2000) – accreditation and validation. The view of the author as the singular origin of a work can support either set of values.

Boundary Objects

A boundary object 'holds different meanings in different social worlds, yet is imbued with enough shared meaning to facilitate its translation across those worlds' (McSherry 2001: 69). As far as present day scientific authorship is concerned, the concept of 'author' itself bridges and reproduces both gift and market economies. Scientific authors, in McSherry's view, can be seen as participating in a system of exchange premised on reciprocity, reputation and responsibility, in which the commodification of scholarship is immoral. Or, to change perspective, they can equally be seen as workers in the academic knowledge economy caught up in a system of capital accumulation and investment, and with their own rights to just reward. Unique origins serves both modes; however many people are involved, as in the Maxwell case, the allocation of different aspects of a work to different authors shows where credit falls. This leads her through some interesting shifts in this relationship over the twentieth century.[17]

The contemporary intensification of debate over the relationship between knowledge and the public good, and how creativity can be pressed into productive use (for the nation reconceived as an economy), is coming to characterise a rather different kind of university from that which occupied most of the twentieth century. We might look for new boundary objects. Are *disciplines* being re-created as boundary objects of a kind? Here the different social worlds they mediate are not those of the gift or commodity, which make authorship so central to both. Rather, disciplines summon divergent routes to creativity – to differently conceived sources of creative energy. Do 'disciplines' these days lead us as much towards undivided outcomes as they do towards undivided origins?

Disciplines are ways of keeping distinct the origins not just of ideas and materials, but of work practices, lines of authentication and accountability. Like originary authorship, their distinctness is a fiction but a convenient one. So do disciplines need individual authors, authenticating agents by virtue of their unique originating status, like ancestors who produce recognisable children? But the genetic metaphor shifts us into a new set of thoughts about creativity. Do disciplines –

instead, also – need collaborators, audiences, co-disciplines: like spouses in search of partners, who produce unique children that match neither parent but become their own sources of vitality? The contrast is between sustaining lineal identities, so that what created the parents also creates the children, and procreating identities out of intermixings because the parents are of mixed origin. The actual kinship system that the English operate – and it is hardly unique in this – manages to deal with both sets of concepts side by side.

In a literary commentary on Gerard Manley Hopkins, who was fascinated with evolutionism and in the 1880s joined Maxwell as a contributor to the journal *Nature,* Beer (1986: 257–8) writes as follows:

> So my argument here is not a matter of finding single sources, or of simply assigning priorities (though I do seek to establish the reading of particular and hitherto undiscussed works and their significance in Hopkins's creativity). As important is feeling the energy available to Hopkins in the scientific, secular world around him, and in which he participated.

Postscript: Boundary Objects do not imply Bounded Objects

It is common in some anthropological thinking to jump to the conclusion that whenever one talks of boundaries, one is talking about what must be enclosed, bounded, within them. The idea of boundary objects is quite other: they are entitles at the borders of discourses, that is, entities which set up borders in themselves, but do not presuppose that a border is also an enclosure.

The issue is relevant to anthropology in so far as cultural borders are so often regarded as setting up boundaries that turn cultures into bounded objects. The notion would have been foreign to the anthropological heirs of the nineteenth-century thinking that imagined culture in the singular,[18] but it grips much of what goes for an anthropological understanding of the present world. It is salutary in this regard to recall boundary objects and discussions elsewhere that emphasise the traffic of cultural values, of concepts, and of intellectual products, without presupposing enclosures and territories. I am thinking particularly of the vocabulary that has sprung up around the notion of transactions across disciplinary 'divides'. Hirsch (forthcoming) has laid some of this out in his discussion of negotiations between domains (after Rabinow) and of Galison's notion of 'trading zones', where mediating languages (pidgins) themselves spring up.[19] To this extent, the zone emerges with a distinctive social character.

The relevance for the present Working Paper is found in a comment about such spaces or zones applied back to the notion of cultures in the plural. James Weiner (n.d.) takes up a discussion of the 'recognition space' between Australian and Aboriginal law – a space in which each party *recognises* the other's space. (In common parlance, recognition and respect here serve somewhat like trade or transaction in liberalising boundaries.) Recognition space already implies, Weiner argues, the notion of a culture with a boundary round it, so each is seen as a bounded object occupying a specific (conceptual) area. That view is simply not tenable for any purposes of analysis we might wish to pursue: ontologically, one cannot distinguish between a difference that emerges within a culture as opposed to a difference that emerges between two cultures. 'Why not start', he says, 'with "one world", wherein peoples, languages and more-or-less well understood "laws" contingently and praxically exist, and posit as our subject matter the differentiating activity that emerges from it and results in such categories as "indigenous" and "non-indigenous"?' (n.d.: 3). The work of differentiation is thus against a backdrop of a field co-extensive with (anyone's) experience. To recover undivided origins or undivided outcomes would here appear to be projects 'after' differentiation.

NOTES

Acknowledgements: Warm thanks to Mary Jacobus, to Kate Price for her commentary, and to Gillian Beer for the central stimulation of her work. Beate Perrey persuaded me to open the paper for further discussion at the CRASSH conference convened by Gillian Beer, Malcolm Bowie and Beate Perrey, 'New Languages for criticism: In(ter)discipline', September 2003. I am grateful to Eric Hirsch for a comment on Working Paper One that stimulated the postscript to Working Paper Two, and to James Weiner for permission to cite his unpublished paper.

1 Stocking 1987; Burton and White 1987. Network autocorrelation analysis was subsequently devised to measure the effects of linkages between societies.

2 The 'connections' (missing links) they pursued were instead those of the investigator trying to make sense – i.e. the investigator had to make connections between apparently isolated (unique) pieces of data. The position of the evolutionists is exemplified by Darwin, and Beer (1996: 29) brings us back to the specificity of his thinking. Darwin, she writes, does away with the sexual pair as an initiating origin: 'the originary parental dyad is figured as the one, sexually undifferentiated – and irretrievable: "the single progenitor"'.

3 Post cold war, post Bayh-Dole (the 1980 Act in the USA that allowed research institutions to have first claim to patent rights in inventions that came from public research funding).

4 Thus 'undivided outcomes' means not that different voices in a team should submerge their distinctiveness, but that orientation to a joint project ('problem solving' etc.) takes precedence. Clearly there are 'communal' and other perceptions of collective ownership, in the case of academic knowledge often linked to ideas about the commons or about the public domain, that fly in the face of the notions described here. I do not venture now into this uneven terrain (cf. Hirsch & Strathern forthcoming).

5 I have not done justice to Beer's account of Maxwell's 'serious merriment', and his literary and poetic finesse with words. 'Maxwell had an unusual spatial capacity in his thought that allows him to hold geometry, poetry, logic, statistics, and joke alongside each other without seeking resolution or hierarchy' (1996: 310).

6 And she tells (Beer 1996: 309) of how he tried to avoid the epistemological temptation to merge the procedures by which a theory is formed with the theory that is formed (e.g. the branching model of evolution – see above comments re connections). Mathematical symbols helped prevent a slide into imitative form.

7 In order to make the exposition clearer, but in fact making it more difficult for the reader to follow the connections, Maxwell divided aspects of his general theory into separate chapters by discipline.

8 Not the only modality. Interpretation involving other interpreters (other authors, respondents) often leads to shifts in voice. Thus the field anthropologist's text may well shift almost imperceptibly from the perspective *of* his or her subjects to a view *on* them.

9 Beer (1996: 150) describes how in the same year (1873) Maxwell was faced with having to describe 'molecules' to the British Association for the Advancement of Science, a new concept for something that could not be seen or held. On his 'wrestling with representation', see Beer 1996: 306–9.

10 Routh had beaten Maxwell into second place in the 1854 mathematical tripos. See below on 'like selves'.

11 'The collective' does not however necessarily correspond to the unified field Maxwell sought: at the outset, at least, teachers at different sites offered different versions of the book's contents. 'The coherent field of theoretical and experimental study envisaged by Maxwell . was thus fragmented through pedagogical expediency into three separate projects [mathematics, physical theory, electrical metrology]' (Warwick 2003: 142).

2 Apparently Caird could not produce manuscripts of his own lectures for the subsequent hearing, but several witnesses attested to the fact that the notes deviated quite a bit from the lectures as they recalled them. The question arose as to whether these notes were, then, really 'reproductions' of the lectures, though such had been Brown's intention (McSherry 2003: 120–1).

13 McSherry quotes Lury's (1993) argument that the discursive production of the author as an autonomnous creator was related to the construction of an abstract audience separate from the creator. The general public became passive consumers whose task was to receive the products of the university rather than evaluate the educational process. This is the position turned on its head by current expectations about public dissemination and stakeholder involvement. See Working Paper Four.

14 The student was in effect upbraided for seeking financial gain (by selling the notes) – he should profit intellectually, not financially, from the contract.

15 She elucidates a central paradox here. On the one hand, if university teachers are to appear, as they did for much of the twentieth century, as arbiters of true knowledge, then an independent academia is best held outside the realm of commodity production and commerce; on the other hand, intellectual property regimes (copyright and, mutatis mutandis, patent laws), by which many academics pursue their 'autonomy', define creative works as commodities and academic workers as owners (McSherry 2001: 103).

16 She cites Star and Griesemer 1989 and Fujimura 1992.

17 Tremendous boundary work once went into representing the academy as a realm of non-property over and against the equation of academic freedom with authorial rights (2001: 7).

18 See, for example, the arguments in Kuper 2000, and his vigorous extension of them (2003).

19 He quotes Rabinow (1996) on negotiations between domains. For a mention of the way Galison's notion has informed the work of Nowotny and her colleagues, see Endnote to this collection.

REFERENCES

Biagioli, M. 2000 'Right or rewards? Changing contexts and definitions of scientific authorship', *Journal of College and University Law* 27: 83–108.

Biagioli, M. and Galison, P. (eds) 2003 *Scientific Authorship: Credit and Intellectual Property in Science*, New York: Routledge.

Barron, A. 1998 'No other law? Author-ity, property and Aboriginal art', in L. Bently and S. Mariatis (eds), *Intellectual Property and Ethics*, London: Sweet and Maxwell.

Beer, G. 1983 *Darwin's Plots: Evolutionary Narrative in Darwin, George Eliot and Nineteenth-Century Fiction*, London: Routledge.

Beer, G. 1996 *Open Fields: Science in Cultural Encounter*, Oxford: Clarendon Press.

Burton, M. and White, D.R. 1987 'Cross-cultural surveys today', *Annual Review of Anthropology* 16: 143–60.

Fujimura, J. 1992 'Crafting science: Standarized packages, boundary objects and translation', in A Pickering (ed.), *Science as Practice and Culture*, Chicago: University of Chicago Press.

Fuller, S. 1996 'Talking metaphysical turkey about epistemological chicken, and the poop on pidgins', in P. Galison and D. Stump (eds) *The Disunity of Science: Boundaries, Contexts and Power*, Stanford, Stanford University Press.

Galison, P. 1996 'Computer simulation and trading zones', in P. Galison and D. Stump (eds) *The Disunity of Science: Boundaries, Contexts and Power*, Stanford, Stanford University Press.

Hirsch, E. (forthcoming) 'Boundaries of creation: The work of credibility in science and ceremony', in E. Hirsch and M. Strathern (eds) *Transactions and Creations: Property Debates and the Stimulus of Melanesia*, Oxford: Berghahn Books.

Hirsch, E. and Strathern, M. (eds) (forthcoming) *Transactions and Creations: Property Debates and the Stimulus of Melanesia*, Oxford: Berghahn Books.

Kuper, A. 1999 *Culture: The Anthropologist's Account*, Cambridge, M.A.: Harvard University Press.

Kuper, A. 2003 'Return of the native', *New Humanist* 118 (3): 22–5.

Lury, C. 1993 *Cultural Rights: Technology, Legality and Personality*, London: Routledge.

McSherry, Corynne 2001 *Who Owns Academic Work? Battling for Control of Intellectual Property*, Cambridge, Mass.: Harvard University Press.

Star, S. and Griesemer, J. 1989 'Institutional ecology, "translations", and boundary objects: Amateurs and professionals in Berkeley's Museum of Vertebrate Technology, 1907–39', *Social Studies of Science* 19: 387–420.

Stocking, G. 1987 *Victorian Anthropology*, New York: The Free Press.

Warwick, Andrew 2003 '"A very hard nut to crack": Making sense of Maxwell's *Treatise on Electricity and Magnetism* in mid-Victorian Cambridge', in M. Biagioli and P. Galison (eds), *Scientific Authorship: Credit and Intellectual Property in Science*, New York: Routledge.

Weiner, James n.d. 'Anthropology, the law and the recognition space', prepared for session 'Articulating culture: understanding engagements between indigenous and non-indigenous life-worlds', Australian Anthological Society conference, Canberra, 2002.

From: 'Making waves: Literary studies in an interdisciplinary context', a conference in honour of Gillian Beer, convened by Mary Jacobus and colleagues, July 2003, Cambridge. I spoke under the rubric 'Open Fields', after the title of one of Beer's collections of essays on science and literature.

WORKING PAPER THREE

Who Owns Academic Knowledge?

Intellectual property debates have ceased to be the domain of lawyers, and, in the academy at least, give rise to many pressing questions. Yet if, as it is claimed, the concept of intellectual property is in crisis, what does that do to universities' and academics' newly asserted rights in the matter? Can one even talk of ownership of knowledge? A social anthropologist stands for a lay interest in the fate of authorship.

Preface to a Conversazione at the British Academy[1]

We have chosen a question that is at once obvious, and not so obvious. The two of us are divided in fact on whether the question is worth asking at all. But we thought there might be some mileage in considering it at this moment in time – given everything that is going on in universities. Hence the rubric: academic *knowledge. This leads us to focus on knowledge produced in an institutional setting, that is, already made complex in relation to diverse interests. It also leads us to consider the role of the universities in the knowledge economy – issues of access and control more often than not lie behind the compulsion to define who owns* the stuff. *And because we are dealing with* knowledge – *rather than with the expression or form of a work – both of us end up talking more about the scientific community than the one broadly represented here. But that is not without general interest.*

One Side of the Debate

Let me start with a short story.

Patents are designed to expire, but once an outfit has made the colossal effort of filing for a patent, not many get withdrawn. One of the very few ever withdrawn concerned blood cells infected with a virus that appeared to confer resistance to leukaemia. Derived from a young man of Hagahai in Papua New Guinea, interest in any potential benefit to come from future investigations involving the infected cells was assigned to the US Department of Health, which had carried out the work of creating a cell-line.[2] The patent led to widespread protest, the US Government being accused, among other things, of 'patenting a man' and, by extension, a population: in the emotional language of one NGO, the patent made no provision for the Hagahai people to receive compensation 'for [their genetic identity] becoming the property of the US Government'.

Among the inventors named in the patent was the medical anthropologist who had sent the blood to an NIH lab in Washington; she subsequently claimed that she had put her name there as a way of protecting the interests of the indigenous people from whom the material had come, that is, she would be the conduit for any future returns to them. Since apparently she had not told a soul that this was her intention – least of all the PNG government – public scepticism may have been justified. At any rate, even though she was formally exonerated, international clamour led to the patent being withdrawn and to the anthropologist leaving the country. The case might have turned out differently if she had been *required* at the outset to declare her interest to the publicly funded medical institute in PNG at which she worked, in other words, had there been a presumption that the institute owned the researcher's intellectual outputs.

Particularly close to home for me, in March 2003 a new Cambridge University Report into intellectual property rights – IPR – was announced, following large scale battle over the University's declared intention to assert 'ownership of all intellectual property generated by its employees in the normal course of their duties'.[3] (The surprise here is that it was the only major UK university which did not.) But if, in one context, ownership seems central, in another it may seem a distraction.

A month later the Royal Society published its radical plea, *Keeping Science Open*.[4] The driving concern of this policy document is how to promote 'the free and rapid flow of information' (1.1) from which new knowledge is generated (1.9). It looks to academia to encourage 'an environment where IP is exploited appropriately and benefits are shared equitably' – and would like to relegate the actual question of ownership to second place (2.8). Yet again, also in April 2003, the Publishers' Association[5] organised a one day conference on the very topic of 'ownership and control' of intellectual assets in the academy, although the rubrics managed to avoid speaking of knowledge as such.[6] And in early May I was at a public discussion on 'who owns the bones'[7] – the challenge that some indigenous descendants of deceased persons put to museum curators: you might think this was a far cry from IP until you reflect that the scientific argument for retention turns on the knowledge that may be extracted from them the bones, which ipso facto would belong, as knowledge, to the extractors thereof.

The sheer plethora and complexity of the issues leads to an admission: it is not only that this or that term of debate is problematic, there are situations where *all of them are*.

For example, it has been argued (McSherry 2001) that the so-called 'knowledge economy', which has made universities aware of IPR, challenges not only the academy *but also* IPR at the same time.[8] IPR, we are told, is in a far from steady state. Consider patents and the creation of new objects, especially through biotechnology, which both do and do not conform to industrial artefacts, and which problematise the very distinction between discovery and invention. Consider copyright and techniques of reproduction, not least in communications and music, which have opened up new questions involving software designers, programmers and licences to publish. Or consider how intellectual property has contributed to an inflation of international rights discourse, encouraging the idea that cultural creations such as 'custom' could be protected as a property right.[9]

The point is this: You cannot have a public debate without holding *some* of the terms steady[10] – whereas in the real world nothing stays still, and it is likely that the terms with which we speak are not just evolving but *co*-evolving in relation to one another. Hence the necessity of this debate. Each of the terms we have produced for discussion has already been stretched: 'owns', 'academic', 'knowledge'. Each opens up numerous perspectives. Three unstable terms and a fourth ('who?'), which makes a question out of them!

I have wanted to make the context as difficult as possible in order to state my position. This is not just to increase the entertainment. I want to convince you that, despite all these factors, the question is worth asking. That is, I want to turn it into a 'real' one. So how can I convince you of this?

I proceed in two stages. First, touching on each term – owns/academic/knowledge – when they are adjacent to one another, beads on a string, prompts some reflections that I think are worth sharing. But these *are* no more than some diverse reflections. Second, then, I want to suggest that holding them together as a question makes the whole more than its parts.

1 (Owns) Ownership

My reflection on 'ownership' has already been sketched. The issue is where it *becomes* an issue and where it does not.

A case in point is the Royal Society's (RS) recommendation (2.8) that what needs encouraging is the appropriate environment for fair exploitation, 'rather than focusing on who owns the IPR'. This is echoed elsewhere, for instance in reference to IPR cross-licensing – negotiations between commercial interests – where it is almost a mantra that the key is not ownership but access (Hill and Turpin 1995: 145). In the academy, one bar to the free exchange of information is the *anticipation* of laying claim to IP rights, for here the inventor, among other things, has to demonstrate novelty, and novelty is destroyed by public disclosure. The RS (3.39) recommends that universities explore ways in which internal exchange can take place without compromising the criterion of novelty – in other words so that the prospect of IP ownership does not raise its head too early and block the crucial flow of knowledge (3.39).

So the very prospect of ownership can be inhibiting, which is why it is best laid to one side. I find this persuasive, but it brings in mind a comparison from outside this field altogether.

There is another arena of much current debate in which it is argued that one should bypass the question of ownership and focus on the transactions, rights of disposal and other possibilities for action. This is the controversy over bodies and body parts. But what is interesting here – and why I bring it up – is that the argument has to be reiterated over and again *because* the popular verdict would have it otherwise. So, people often assume that when the question of organ donation comes up, that must presuppose ownership – you give away what you have property in. This is despite lawyers saying that the term 'donation' has nothing to do with property ownership, but is instead connected to the fact that invasion of a body is trespass. Common law is concerned with trespass, and donation – like the mobilisation of consent – obviates the illegality of trespass.[11]

But that leads one to ask, what is so troublesome about ownership that one should have to push it to one side? Why is it so tenacious? It would seem that people constantly fall back into thinking about ownership in relation to the body only for lawyers and others to knock down. Are the former clinging to an outworn concept that gets in the way of the real business of dealing with diverse interests? Of course in IPR it is not because ownership is outworn that it can get in the way of the creative generation of knowledge on which innovation depends – it is because it confers an exclusivity to rights over access.

However, I want to leave the obvious point about power and reflect on a less obvious one suggested by the analogy. When something is consistently denied, the denial is bound to be going against the grain. So what would going *with* the grain mean; what are the indigenous assumptions here?

Which bring me to a reflection. In avoiding the term 'ownership', what assumptions are we concealing from ourselves?

One response: Presumably it is all the social justifications that make the ownership of rights a form of property. If what is being pushed to one side is being rendered contingent or incidental, it is the very notion of 'property' itself that makes the denial an extremely interesting form of social critique. And how do academics engage in this critique?

2 Academic

Academic output is the subject of a book by McSherry (then at the Stanford Law School) that was one impetus for this conversazione. Its title is in fact 'Who owns academic *work*'? You might want to ask what mischief is done by putting 'knowledge' in place of 'work'. But the subtitle tells all: 'Battling for control of intellectual property'. And she opens with a case that concerned the leaking of research results through a doctoral student, who channelled information from the lab where she had studied to researchers in a pharmaceutical firm. This example is from the US, of course, and her cases are largely informed by the hierarchies of academics – juniors against seniors. The conflicts there involved law suits, not just debates.

But what precisely is debatable about academic outputs, as opposed to other kinds? Well, consider this: it is here that we encounter the reverse of coyness about ownership. There are many contexts in which academics are *urged* to treat their output as something to be owned. Property rights over what they create should be made evident.[12]

The urging comes from the Government and its agencies, and it is not the individual academics but their institutions that are exhorted to behave as owners.[13] There is a strongly voiced argument that universities should be treating public funding as investment, returning profits to the taxpayer and regenerating the material base of innovation by ploughing finances back into more research. The assertion of property title in intellectual output is a way of ensuring this. Now, to appreciate why universities themselves have to be *urged* to seek this form of property requires some historical context. Namely that the historical *denial of ownership* in academia was a social critique that had become ingrained as orthodoxy.[14]

McSherry is concerned largely with science (in the US), and she argues that, insofar as the twentieth-century research university developed as the primary producer of science, it was most useful to commerce and government in its apparent independence from them. Its role, to validate the autonomy of scientific facts, found a social form in an autonomous community of scholars – where it became 'inappropriate to identify one's creations as private property' (McSherry 2001: 74–5).[15] Individual 'ownership' was antithetical to this ethos.

These days that has been turned on its head, and in the UK as well as the US. Divisions between the market and the academy are blurred by increasing pressure to bring intellectual protection into the scholarly reward system. Previously separable domains are not as discrete as they were once imagined to be. But the situation is also turned on its side: there is a new stakeholder in knowledge production – a collective or corporate individual, not the community of scholars but the institution which employs them. More strongly than that, as we have seen, there is a positive duty for bodies such as universities to protect investment in them, and that is on grounds that they are publicly funded institutions.[16] So the university's private interests are also public ones.

In the UK, publicly funded Research Councils *oblige* the universities, as the relevant public bodies, to take on the ownership of intellectual property created in the course of research. Note the double public duty: to disseminate knowledge, which is what patents encourage; and to return public investment by allocating IPR to the university. Cambridge University presents its assertion of claims of ownership as a way of making sure benefits are to 'society'.[17] But as the Royal Society paper asks (1.7), 'Which society?'[18]

Reflection: can there be a *duty* of ownership, and is it one which academic employment is specifically justified in imposing?

3 Who

This is the point at which to insert the interrogative, 'who?'

The pressures of the 'knowledge economy' are evident. Now, McSherry is interested in why this should be *represented* as a crisis. She considers what work crisis rhetoric does and would probably say that asking the very question '*Who* owns academic knowledge?' is a kind of crisis-fixing ('fix' as in repair).[19] For example: focusing on what is thought of as public and private allows for surface negotiations while leaving underlying assumptions intact.[20] In the case of IPR, one underlying assumption is that the natural compensation for creative effort is property ownership. So long as that assumption is in place, a crisis can be managed by preserving existing 'balances' between private and public interests in the market place of ideas. Even if it is distributed between different players, it seems there is an answer to 'who owns?' But the answer has, as it were, already narrowed down 'society'. By considering the public good *in the context of* private property interests, society appears in the guise of the specific provider to whom the receiver of funds becomes accountable. Society as a generalised and grateful beneficiary of 'knowledge' has to find a voice through other means.

There are interesting side-effects to the clamour for staking claims. A climate of heightened consciousness over ownership of rights in intellectual outputs – in which academics are urged to acknowledge links to industry – raises obvious questions about who the appropriate holder of the rights is. Indeed, it is actually possible to debate whether it is the institution or the inventor/creator which should lay claims to ownership. Curious, since you would have thought that IPR law in relation to the obligations of employment had sorted this out long ago. It has, in the case of universities, but through an interesting exceptionalism. This concerns scientists and non-scientists alike.

Patents are only one part of what may be owned. Academics can be other kinds of owners of rights.

It has been accepted by the Court of Appeal that academic work at universities is based on assumptions different from that imposed by other employer–employee agreements. More than that, it is acknowledged that there is a special connection between an academic and his or her work that actually requires *protection from* the institution. Here the institution is very much in its private guise, for it is feared that with control over intellectual output it might suppress what it did not favour. (In time-honoured manner, presumably, it would seek to suppress sedition: the dissemination of, in its eyes, potentially dangerous, distasteful or even, in these times of Research Assessment Exercises, mediocre information.) And here copyright steps in to protect the author. No one contests the *who*: it is generally presumed that university staff own copyright in their publications, papers and lecture notes, a by-product being another way of conserving the flow of ideas[21] (Report to Cambridge University on Copyright 2001: 4.1.1).

Traditionally, the academic may not have wished to create private property out of his or her output, but he or she may have wished to exercise something akin to *personal* ownership.

Reflection: who is protecting what from whom?

4 Knowledge

Underlying all this: what is this 'knowledge'? Why have we used the term? Perhaps because it draws attention to that kind of personal investment in work.

Now, one of the arguments about ring-fencing copyright from the interests of the university is based on the intimate relationship imagined between the author and his or her work. Regardless of the fact that the legal association is simply one of 'origin' – who, technically speaking, is the source of the work – the popular assumption for years has been that the originator is the creator, and that accreditation is at once a matter of reward and acknowledgement. Here I want you to consider an interesting situation (familiar to you, the reader).

Scientists have used the term 'gift exchange' for a prestige-reward system through which scientists both ensure the circulation of information, and gain recognition for doing so.[22] The individual supposedly shares findings with the scientific community at large, so that knowledge taken out of a public domain is returned to it.[23] Unless scientific findings have circulated among co-researchers, they cannot be verified: truths about the world must become facts in a public domain. 'Scientists buttress their new claims by connecting them as much as possible to the body of previous scientific literature' (Biagioli 2000: 88). Practitioners are accountable to one another.

Now, what is fascinating is the argument that the logic of an intellectual property system is actually antithetical to this kind of accreditation.[24] The contrast is both with patents, which are about utility rather than the factual status of scientific knowledge, and with copyright, which is about original expression, a veritable distraction to truth claims that need to be based on commonly shared agreements. IPR does not deal with these aspects of knowledge. Indeed, what is being called *knowledge* in this context is defined by its belonging to a person, albeit a collective person, an academic 'community' – a community that is not at all the same as the university. In turn, the community will be defined by the knowledge it possesses.

This way of understanding knowledge is, I would suggest, similar to that behind the popular association of copyright with the personal investment of the creator of the work. Knowledge – as opposed to information (say) – points to the way persons make facts, data, or whatever, belong to themselves.[25] In the same way, the words or the image or whatever is being protected in copyright involves questions of identity, not just identification, and points to the author's personality. What is equally fascinating, therefore, is to see a comparable split between IPR proper and this domain of personal authorship.

Indeed 'authorship' in this latter sense may have to be *protected from* copyright claims! In recent years there has been a move to distinguish economic rights from moral rights: a distinction between (a) the ownership of rights in an intellectual resource (IPR), a contractual and legal matter; and

(b) the assertion of 'moral rights', the right to be named as author (recognition, accreditation and so forth). The economic rights can be bought and sold; the moral rights are tied to the author as originator. The two sets of rights-holders may coincide, but need not.[26]

What is interesting is that, regardless of what is happening in IPR, there is a seeming need for accreditation.[27] And I want to suggest that this is welcome on one ground at least. The obverse of accreditation is accountability. The author who is named is the author who is responsible. Whether it is for vouching for the validity of information, or in defence of a particular argument, the work is traceable. And it is traceable to someone with a social identity – whether as an avowed member of a scholarly community or not.

Reflection: a focus on knowledge enables us to ask the question – what kind of social person is the author?

Conclusion

We might ponder on the four points for reflection:

1 Ownership: In avoiding the term ownership, what assumptions are we concealing from ourselves?
2 Academic: Can there be a duty of ownership, and is it one which academic employment is specifically justified in imposing?
3 Who: Who is protecting what from whom?
4 Knowledge: What kind of social person is the author?

Some food for discussion, I hope. Although separately they dart off in all directions, is there anything that we might wish to keep stable in all this? I want to end with just one position, for myself.

I said I wanted to convince you that, even with all the caveats about how changing and multi-referenced the terms are, the simple question posed by the topic of this conversazione is worth asking. Rather than focusing on the individual terms, I want to take the question a whole: it is as *a whole question* that it has some useful work to do. That is because of something I propose to share with you that touches me directly.

Remember the Hagahai case at the beginning. I distanced it from myself: it was about a biological, not a social anthropologist; about US involvement, not UK; and about patents, not the kind of concerns over accreditation that might affect a social anthropologist like myself.

I should bring the issue closer to home. Not long ago I had a letter from a good friend and knowledge-expert from Mt. Hagen, Papua New Guinea, a significant 'field' for my researches since 1964, who posed a question to me. It was addressed in an indirect, elliptical way (and I disguise it a little further). When a woman goes in marriage to another clan, and bears many children for that clan, the writer asked, will her in-laws think on the kin from which she came? When someone plants a seedling, and that seedling grows into a tree, and the tree bears much fruit, will the eater of the fruit think on the person who planted the seedling? 'Thinking on' is an orientation to another person that is meant to summon all the strands of obligation and mutual acknowledgement/recompense that put people into one another's debt. The reference was clearly to intellectual property, as the university teacher who typed the letter spelled out in a covering note.

What the writer means is *knowledge* – everything that I have gleaned. What he means is *academic* knowledge – the knowledge gleaned to further the reputation of the institution as well as the individual. What he means is *owns* – who has it in their possession, controls its disposition and claims authority to use it, even possibly to sell. And the question is of course all about *who*. What he was not complaining about was that I had this in my possession to use. He was not complaining that I had turned into academic knowledge something that existed in other forms (appropriation through labour/technology) – he had no problem about that having been done. No challenge to any 'rights' in the matter.

The question he was putting in front of me was the question of responsibility, of moral authorship if you like. The question was of equitable reward. Not a determination of who has the rights, but of how we were going to conduct our relationship. I had to declare my 'ownership', in the sense of making an admission of accountability, precisely in order for him to put the counterclaim. Well, what about the person who planted the seedling? The outcome did not imply singular ownership – on the contrary, it opened up the issue to non-exclusive interests – but it did imply claiming an association that would allow one to see, to render visible, everyone else who was also associated with the process.

Not so different from the Hagahai after all, except that Carol Jenkins actually did something about it. She claimed that having her name there among the 'inventors' of the cell line was the only responsible way in which she could protect the future interests of the Hagahai people (Strathern 2004: 77). In signing her name with the intention that they would receive her share of any royalties that might accrue, she specifically saw this as a form of return for their participation in the research.

Final reflection: The simple question is worth asking, that is, the whole question in its entirety, and it is important to go on with the asking. It reminds us of the social world in which we live.

And so I arrive at the position that 'ownership' has at least one valuable job to do. Its value is precisely because it is open to contest: it puts the form of identity an academic might claim in relation to his or her work into a field of identities, a network of social actors with their overlapping claims on 'the owner'. When the owner is declared, their relationships with all those who have supported them can also be declared. Not asserting anything primordial or unchallengeable, in this guise, at least, it (ownership) *invites* further questions.[28]

ANNEX

A Comparison[29]

A comparison comes to mind: debates over appropriations from 'culture'.

Many of the concerns of the international cultural property debate, as it affects 'indigenous peoples' and 'traditional cultures', echo the property/commons nexus found in Euro-American discourse on scientific knowledge. Rather like the perceived autonomy of scholars, and the assumption of community, peoples with 'cultures' (especially 'indigenous', 'third world' and 'first nations' peoples) are imagined as collective or communal entities with generalised public-domain ethics. What exactly is the parallel? Crudely, knowledge belongs to (can be claimed by) communities near and far. The near one of scientists contrasts with the far one of a universal beneficiary, 'mankind'; both ordinarily lie beyond property. Similarly, cultural products belong both to their culture of origin and to world heritage, as a kind of non-exclusive, distributable resource. Resources of 'near' communities only become commodifiable if they are turned into items outsiders will value (patentable inventions, tourist art); but anything can be a potential resource for these 'far' ones. The debate is what kind of protection property rights offer or require. For scientific and cultural authorship alike, Euro-Americans can thus ask whether property rights *assist* protection or whether protection is needed *from* them.

It does not take much to see the uses served to industrial nations by the notion of open-access culture. Resources existing in some kind of public domain, if not terra nullius – outside prior property claims – are seemingly available to all (e.g. Brush 1999: 540). Beside this, the perceived autonomy of 'traditional culture' puts a certain political, if not neo-colonial, stamp on developing countries or ethnic minorities. The private/public debate over access to scientific information, and how private rights are established to what otherwise circulates freely, are precisely the concerns of the cultural property debate as to who does or does not have rights (and what can or cannot be commodified) in traditional knowledge or shared customs.

An underlying assumption in both cases is that appropriation means something private is made out of what – if left to circulate unhindered – would circulate in a public domain. The private/public debate over access to scientific information, then, and how property rights are established to what otherwise should circulate freely, is replicated in the concerns of the cultural property lobby as to who does or does not have rights (and what can or cannot be commodified) in traditional knowledge or shared customs. Some of the critiques of this lobby I would see as examples of McSherry's 'crisis-fixing'. We should be questioning the assumptions. What work does a public/private, individual/communal rhetoric do?

NOTES

Acknowledgements: Warm thanks to Ru Kundil for his teaching. I am also grateful for the impetus of Alain Pottage's contribution to the Conversazione, although this is not the only part of his work on which I have drawn with profit. The topic takes forward discussions developed under the auspices of PTC, 'Property, Transactions and Creations: New Economic Relations in the Pacific', an investigation co-convened with Eric Hirsch and funded by the UK Economic and Social Research Council, 1999–2002 (award R000 23 7838). For several comments, during and after the event, many thanks – in particular to John Enderby (The Royal Society) and Michael Brown (Cavendish Laboratories, Cambridge). Finally, the British Academy and the Conversazione convenor,

Margaret Boden, must be acknowledged – both for the original idea and for their subsequent hospitality.

1 The preface refers to the two talks given by Marilyn Strathern and Alain Pottage that, with the audience's participation in discussion afterwards, made up the Conversazione. These are relatively informal occasions. Speakers are expected to furnish material for debate and thus to take up distinct stances, if not actually polemical ones. They defend a position, not necessarily their own views. Alain Pottage and I, who probably hold rather similar views in this area, deliberately differentiated ourselves and exaggerated the positions for which we were arguing. This, with some small modifications, is the text of Marilyn Strathern's talk. Pottage's talk is to appear in a subsequent issue of *Cambridge Anthropology*.

2 The virus only grows in human T-cells (anti-bodies) and therefore had to be deposited in a human cell line of this type to be rendered accessible. The patent was filed in 1992, granted in 1995 and withdrawn in 1996. (This is a case on which we have both written: Pottage 1998; Strathern 2001. For a more recent anthropological comment, see Kirsch forthcoming.)

3 In the University's initial statement of intention, IP rights are canonically patents, along with copyright applied to designs and software, while all other copyright is treated as a separate issue outside this jurisdiction. A 2001 report on copyright for the University of Cambridge made it clear that this is no more than the legal situation. The general rule is that university staff own copyright in their works. Note that unlike patents, design rights etc., copyright is created in absence of registration, and would cover *any* writing, notes, speech, artefact which a person produced.

4 Royal Society 2003 *Keeping Science Open: The Effects of Intellectual Property Policy on the Conduct of Science*, Policy Document 02/03, London: The Royal Society. This is sequel to an earlier multilateral review from the National Academies Advisory Group (*Intellectual Property and the Academic Community*, NAPAG, London, 1995).

5 The Publishers' Association and the Department of Journalism, City University, 'Ownership and Control: Managing Intellectual Property Rights in Universities', City University, 28 April 2003.

6 It refers to 'teaching and learning material', '[research] results', 'new assets' etc.

7 'Human Remains: Objects to study or ancestors to bury', The Institute of Ideas and the Royal College of Physicians, RCP, 2 May 2003.

8 The two may even be dramatised as though they were in some kind of *mutual* crisis (Pottage 1998).

9 And, as for the inventiveness of scientists and the certainty of authorship, scientific periodicals try to recognise everyone involved in a piece of research while avoiding being swamped by multi-author citations.

10 Unless you create a forum such as is found at UN document-producing sessions, where it is expected that most of not all the key terms will get bracketed; for extensive discussion see Riles (1998).

11 The body may not be property, and cannot be owned as property, but persons may have a variety of interests in it that be mobilised *while avoiding the question of ownership* (Nuffield Council 1995: 18). While Robertson per contra uses the language of property ownership – frozen embryos as property of gamete providers (1994: 106) and owners of gametes (1994: 28,

104) – he also implies that one can obviate the question of ownership by dispositional agreements. See Davies and Naffine 2001.

12 And everything entailed in establishing the basis to such rights. Hirsch (forthcoming) quotes Rabinow's (1996) famous question of a US scientist, 'Who invented PCR [polymerase chain reaction]?', to which the reply came back: 'Conception, development and application are all scientific issues – invention is a question for the patent lawyers.'

13 In the US this was instituted by what is known as the Bayh-Dole Act after its protagonists (University and Small Business Patent Procedures Act, 1980). It empowers university bodies to hold patents arising from federally sponsored research as a way of demonstrating returns to the taxpayer. Note the timing of this move in the light of international politics: the prospect of military funding for technology research drying up with the end of the Cold War (for a reminder on this point I thank Eric Hirsch, pers.comm; see McSherry 2001: 152).

14 McSherry's argument is that, as least as far as science was concerned, the social critique was sustained by other interests as well, and these were blatantly politico-economic: it was useful to commerce that the university kept its distance from the market.

15 Specifically: 'intellectual property is defined in contradistinction to a conceptual space, namely, the public domain, that is anchored in the United States by the research university' (2001: 27). The market traditionally thrived on the production of information authenticated by being produced independently of it (the commodity creates a 'non-commodity' sphere).

16 McSherry (2001: 2): The ethical management of IPR is declared to be a principal duty of (US) academy.

17 On analogy with the corporation reaping returns from its R & D investment. The 1995 NAPAG Report identified a tendency to pushing boundaries of patenting from invention into the area of knowledge. The trend continues: 'increased public recognition of the key role that patents can play in building corporate value in the "knowledge economy"' (Royal Society 2003: 7).

18 It goes on, the UK, the EU, the World? And it raises the pertinent question of benefits actually accruing to some at the expense of others.

19 If McSherry (2001: 25) argues that IP law is currently represented as in crisis, so too is the university (that each has always been in crisis is no answer). There are various reasons why each is in crisis, but it is not a coincidence that both are. She is interested in the mutually constitutive relationship between IP and the modern research university (2001: 27), particularly in respect of science.

20 An example: Hilgartner (2000: 7) observes that one needs to understand 'the processes that shape what gets made public, what is kept private, and what is deployed in transactions that fall between these extremes'.

21 See n. 3, above. The right of University employees to assert ownership to the copyright in a work 'written, composed or drafted' by them may be interpreted as a part of the employee's implicit contract with the University.

22 Iconically, one gives publications to peers as a gift and receives credit as a counter-gift (Biagioli 2000: 85, quoting Hagstrom 1982). As in the Euro-American 'gift economy' (Cheal 1988), altruism towards the world at large often substitutes for reciprocity.

23 'While the production of value in liberal economy involves a movement between two complementary categories, from generic public domain to spe-

cific private property, in science the movement is within the same category (the public domain) and it goes from "unspecified" to "specified truth"' (Biagioli 2000: 88–9).

24 The rewards of IPR allegedly divide the community. Scientific norms reject the portrayal of data as an individual creation (McSherry 2001: 207). She raises questions about whether the delivery of a lecture should be seen as a solitary act.

25 We all have our definitions of these terms; this is allied to thinking of knowledge as information that a person makes relevant to him or herself. Of course the idea that someone possesses something as knowledge can get built into the justifications for IP. In staking out an IPR claim, researchers have to demonstrate that the work is 'theirs' (lay grounds to authorship of it) – and do so by many other pieces of evidence than simply the fact that it originated with them.

26 This has been overtaken to some extent by explorations of new relations with publishers, e.g. debates over rights to licence, where a similar split (between economic and 'moral' rights) is repeated, but this time with copyright remaining with the author. (See Royal Society Report 2003: 18 and elsewhere.)

27 Which echoes (seventeenth-century) pre-copyright notions of proprietorship, an old view of authorship that has persisted in scientific circles in the need for accountability.

28 Is this a version of the Hegelian position that property gives us a means of entering into contracts with others? We recognise both others and ourselves as owners. ('Property is therefore essential to the formation of social relationships', Davies and Naffine 2001: 4.)

29 The arguments are developed further in the two PTC ('Property Transactions and Creations') volumes: (a) Lawrence Kalinoe and James Leach (eds) 2004, *Rationales of Ownership: Transactions and Claims to Ownership in Contemporary Papua New Guinea*, Wantage: Sean Kingston Publishing; (b) Eric Hirsch and Marilyn Strathern (eds) forthcoming, *Transactions and Creations: Property Debates and the Stimulus of Melanesia*, Oxford: Berghahn.

REFERENCES

Biagioli, M. 2000 'Right or rewards? Changing contexts and definitions of scientific authorship', *Journal of College and University Law* 27: 83–108.

Brush, S. 1999 'Bioprospecting in the public domain', *Cultural Anthropology* 14: 535–55.

Cheal, D. 1988 *The Gift Economy*, London: Routledge.

Davies, M. and Naffine, N. 2001 *Are Persons Property? Legal Debates about Property and Personality*, Aldershot: Ashgate.

Hagstrom, W. O. 1982 'Gift giving as an organising principle in science', in B. Barnes and D. Edge (eds) *Science in Context*, Cambridge, Mass: MIT Press.

Hilgartner, S. 2000 'Access to data and intellectual property: scientific exchange in genome research', *Intellectual Property Rights and Research Tools in Molecular Biology* [http://stills.nap.edu/html/property/4.htm]

Hill, S. and Turpin, T. 1995 'Cultures in collision: The emergence of a new localism in academic research', in M. Strathern (ed.), *Shifting Contexts: Transformations in Anthropological Knowledge*, London: Routledge.

Hirsch, E. [forthcoming] 'Boundaries of creation: the work of credibility in science and ceremony', in E. Hirsch and M. Strathern (eds) *Transactions and Creations: Property Debates and the Stimulus of Melanesia*, Oxford: Berghahn.

Kirsch, S. [forthcoming] 'Property limits', in E. Hirsch and M, Strathern (eds) *Transactions and Creations: Property Debates and the Stimulus of Melanesia*, Oxford: Berghahn.

McSherry, C. 2001 *Who Owns Academic Work? Battling for Control of Intellectual Property*, Cambridge, Mass.: Harvard University Press.

NAPAG (National Academies Policy Advisory Group) 1995 *Intellectual Policy and the Academic Community*, London: The Royal Society.

Nuffield Council 1995 *Human Tissue: Ethical and Legal issues*, London: Nuffield Council on Bioethics.

Pottage, A. 1998 'The inscription of life in law: genes, parents, and bio-politics', *Modern Law Review* 61: 740–65.

Riles, A. 1998 'Infinity within the brackets', *American Ethnologist* 25: 378–98.

Rabinow, P. 1996 *Making PCR. A Story of Biotechnology.* Chicago: University of Chicago Press.

Robertson, J. 1994 *Children of Choice: Freedom and the New Reproductive Technologies*, Princeton, NJ: Princeton University Press.

Royal Society 2003 *Keeping Science Open: The Effects of Intellectual Property Policy on the Conduct of Science*, Policy Document 02/03, London: The Royal Society.

Strathern, M. 2004 'Global and local contexts', in L. Kalinoe and J. Leach (eds), *Rationales of Ownership: Transactions and Claims to Ownership in Contemporary Papua New Guinea*, Wantage: Sean Kingston Publishing.

From: British Academy Conversazione, "Who owns academic knowledge?", Marilyn Strathern and Alain Pottage, London, The British Academy, May 2003. This comes from the text first published in *Cambridge Anthropology*, 23: 1 – 17, 2003. Permission to reproduce is gratefully acknowledged.

WORKING PAPER FOUR
Accountability Across Disciplines

Disciplines have an in-built accountability of a kind (self-monitoring and epistemological, i.e. knowing how knowledge is made and where it comes from). The issues for cross-disciplinary work then become precisely how one 'measures' what one is doing, whether it is a question of validation ('proving' findings against one another) or knowing who one's audience is going to be (how well messages have been communicated) or how to assess the value of a product or output (assessing a hybrid). My question would be whether or not these would be interesting issues to think through via a model of 'accountability', and what different models of accountability they might prompt.

The Centre National de la Recherche Scientifique has a discussion on its website at the moment on the topic of interdisciplinarity.[1] This is obviously the culmination of extensive earlier debate across disciplines (social scientists, philosophers, historians, anthropologists and cognitive scientists are invoked). It aims to get approximately a paper a month online. The anthropologist cum cognitivist Dan Sperber started the series off in April 2003; the next month Helga Nowotny, from Social Studies of Science, one of the authors of *The New Production of Knowledge* (Gibbons *et al.* 1994) and its sequel *Re-thinking Science* (2001), presented 'The potential of transdisciplinarity'. I am a latecomer to the topic –

and still have to inform myself of it and its history. So why get involved at all?

Interdisciplinarity Everywhere

It is perennially interesting to ask why subjects which have been around for a long time, and interdisciplinarity must have emerged at the same time as disciplines became formalised, suddenly seem of the moment. Why must it be *seen* to be on everyone's agenda; why its new visibility?[2]

Of course interdisciplinarity has been long with us – not least in the phenomenon of centres that often co-ordinate both research and non-research interests. Sitting alongside university departments, such centres have everywhere taken hold as well established features of the academic landscape. At the same time there seems something new here: 'interdisciplinarity' as a totalising mode of academic being is undergoing hyper-formalisation. Explicitly on the agenda of *all* the UK Research Councils (see DTI 2001a, 2001 b), interdisciplinarity will no doubt be flagged at the next Research Assessment Exercise. Away from centres with a largely research or co-ordinating function, it appears as the rationale for re-grouping departments and inspires re-conceptualisations of teaching disciplines.[3] Again, and especially in the natural sciences, re-grouping as such has been occurring for years.[4] But the re-grouping of disciplines is not enough: interdisciplinary effort must also be made explicit.

An example: the physical sciences in Cambridge have just (as of April 2003) formalised an Interdisciplinary Research Network (UCIRN).[5] And by formalised, I mean that the network is funded, it will hold seminars and symposia in its name, it will be under a network management team, with an advisory committee, while the day-to-day running of the network will be under a network director responsible to the network research facilitator. The last is the new Plummer Professor of Chemical and Structural Biology, a post held jointly in the Departments of Chemistry, Physics and Biochemistry, 'a post designed explicitly to promote interdisciplinarity and interdepartmental collaboration within the University'. It is not sufficient to wait, so to speak, for collaborative needs to arise in the solving of specific 'problems' (problems within biology that may be investigated within the context of physics is given as an example) but interdisciplinarity must be actively pursued in all directions (so that the way in which biological problems are amenable to physical description becomes drawn into the science itself). One set of aims is to engage disciplines 'not traditionally linked through standard research practices', and to simulate 'new collaborations across the University'. Another set concerns the desirability of setting up a knowledge base that will itself be widely available and therefore make scientific findings widely available. Among other things, this will serve as a repository for papers, in some cases written by the network managers, designed to demystify complex areas of science, 'thereby making them accessible to a wide [scientific] audience'. The accompanying bureaucratic structure, we may note, makes the need for management evident.

If we take management as an index of visibility, we are led back to the question of why interdisciplinary effort must, in this way at least, be made visible and explicit.

Transdisciplinarity

Let me go back to the website discussion of Nowtny's notion of transdisciplinarity. The point of the new word is to convey the work of new thinking (see Gibbons *et al.* 1994: 27–30).[6] In parenthesis, I remark that I follow usage where it is found, and do not myself make any analytical distinction between the elements of this mouth-filling trio (multi-, inter- and trans-disciplinarily). I take the distinctions as indigenous classifications.

For Nowotny the differences are crucial. Multidisciplinarity, the alignment of skills from different disciplines, is left behind. She advocates a kind of super-interdisciplinarity. That is, transdisciplinarity brings disciplines together in contexts where new approaches arise out of the interaction between them, but to a heightened degree. The focus is on its context of application, and on a particular approach to problem-solving that creates its own theoretical impetus. Interdisciplinarity may involve a common framework, shared across disciplines which each contribute their bit. But transdisciplinarity, in this definition, requires 'a common theoretical understanding' and a 'mutual interpenetration of disciplinary epistemologies' (Gibbons *et al.* 1994: 29). And it does not just disrespect disciplinary boundaries – it disrespects institutional ones too.[7] In other words, the reach into core disciplinary practices carries the expectation of new theoretical models and new institutional forms.

Here two things happen to this interesting argument, summarised succinctly in the online paper (Nowotny 2003). First is the claim that what is happening in disciplines is also happening in society at large – a breakdown of functional differences between separate domains of social life, and the emergence of multi-tasking skills, diversified companies and, in the form of bodies such as NGOs, 'ways in which various kinds of stakeholders organise in shaping social reality'. But what initially appears as an analogy then takes the form of an organic dovetailing – of convergence or co-evolution, in her words. For the society that is also changing becomes itself a factor in the production of knowledge, and its interventions form one of the platforms for the new applications of knowledge. Engaging thus with society creates a 'context of application', with the rider that 'the context speaks back'.[8] And, Nowotny adds, the context of implication, with the rider that questions about the (social) implications of scientific practice, must first be asked 'in the scientific laboratories', recognising that the question will be answered in multiple ways. Only in this manner will scientifically reliable knowledge also become knowledge that is 'socially robust'. To echo Corinne Hayden (2002), this is one way in which 'society' is imagined as drawn into the scientific enterprise.[9]

However it is the second part of Nowotny's argument I wish to dwell on. The involvement of society, whoever its representatives (Callon 1986) are, signals a diagnostic feature of the new knowledge production.[10] The feature is summed up in one word: accountability. Accountability, as she spells out, is not just a matter of taking on personal responsibilities; it is a formal process of 'institutional responsibility' that must acknowledge the interests of users – there may be multiple users – and acknowledge the user's right to know what is going in the very organisation of knowledge production. 'You know to whom you are accountable. There are certain procedures to make things visible that are otherwise invisible' (Nowotny 2003: 3). In other words, institutional responsibility for output flows into responsibility for (visible) self-management as a (responsible) institution.

There is a parallel rhetorical confluence in how users are conceived, and it was sketched within the scientists' blueprint for an Interdisciplinary Network even though the wider community is that of scientists themselves. The confluence is this: reaching beyond disciplines merges with reaching beyond academia. They appear commensurate virtues. For in either case the key on academia's side is to *manage* knowledge (output) in such a way as to enable its dissemination. Clarity of purpose in dissemination is the first step towards accountability. Dissemination switches the nature of the scientific enterprise of course: the communicable act moves into prominence the relation with the stakeholders, those 'for whom' the research is being done, Nowotny says. And models of communication suggest a two-way flow.[11]

What is happening here? Accountability is being wheeled in as the demonstration that science has taken society into account. At the same time, society, no longer simply the recipient of knowledge, has an input into science.[12] There is a kind of generalised accountability, then, that is served by bringing in outside parties, who at *the level of communication* have a sort of parity. Of course that partnership requires the ideological conservation of distinctness. The non-scientists may be interested parties – but the point is that their interests are distinct from those of the knowledge producers, even if they 'mingle' their knowledge in. The point is familiar to anthropologists: accountability is envisaged as the outcome of a transaction, and it is the transaction itself – science's engagement with society's representatives – which keeps the two sides separate.[13]

In the meantime, I want to point to a third, hidden, confluence. Or perhaps the speed of the riverine image can be reversed – to many marshy streams, so the detritus is not swept away and everything becomes sluggish. Accountability is at once: (1) a moral stance towards the wider world (the 'context' now invited to speak back); and (2) a set of procedures for verification.[14] Greater visibility appears to answer both. But, in the second case, what is verified is performance (Munro 1999), and the detritus of accountability are those systems of performance measurement that accountability must trail behind it. For all that Nowotny and her colleagues see the new transdisciplinarity as changing the very process of knowledge production, welcoming the unknown, making better science and better citizens together,[15] with the potential to break down ('transgress') institutional barriers, all spurred on by a sense of accountability-1, accountability-2, the verification of institutional achievement, can only be demonstrated by

---

Three forms of confluence

1 Analogy between what is happening in disciplines and what is happening in society turns out to be an organic merging – society is drawn into the definition of disciplines (the metaphorical literalised).
2 Institutional responsibility for output flows into responsibility for self-management as a (responsible) institution (reflexivity implemented).
3 Accountability as (1) a moral stance towards the wider world (the 'context' now invited to speak back) is merged with (2) a set of procedures for verification. Either may also encompass the other (merographic relation created).

---

specifying in advance what is going to be measured. Targets and indicators, necessarily, properly, slow everything down.

Models of Accountability

The Cambridge Genetics Knowledge Park (CGKP) is a model for the management of interdisciplinarity.[16] It must also be perplexed by questions of measurement. 'The categorisation of deliverables in an enterprise as novel and complex as a Genetics Knowledge park provides a huge challenge, especially in relation to the definition of outputs and outcomes' (Zimmern 2001).

Initially funded for five years, this simultaneously local and virtual consortium originates in the UK's Department of Health's (DoH) desire, with the Department of Trade and Industry's (DTI) support, to put research in clinical genetics into 'context' (aka Nowotny): bringing together multiple aspects of emerging medical developments, developing a knowledge base, and thereby ensuring their acceptability to the public. The scheme is premised on interaction between several sciences, between scientific and clinical applications, between academic and non-academic users, and between Cambridge and the commercial community.

Of the six national Parks, the Cambridge plan goes furthest in responding to the invitation to 'develop appropriate economic, ethical, legal and social frameworks for the effective delivery of genetic services' (Zimmern 2001). New research will have implications beyond the field of human genetics, and (with regard to accountability) it has become irresponsible not to anticipate that. The CGKP will offer visible evidence of the way society can be taken into science before, so to speak, it leaves the labs. To produce knowledge that will be socially robust is one of its four institutional objectives. This one reads: 'To transform information from scientific studies on genetics into knowledge *through its validation* by critical appraisal, by seeking a patient and public perspective, and by placing it in its ethical, legal and social context' (my emphasis).[17] As the original proposal points out, the process of validation will simultaneously involve disciplines 'not normally included' in the purview of science and 'interpret that science in a wide social context'. As we have already seen, going across disciplines is bracketed with the idea of taking society into account – especially when the disciplines come from the social sciences.[18]

The CGKP is very conscious of its responsibilities towards the DoH and DTI, and of the need for there to be 'deliverables' at the end of the day. It is driven by the formula – inspired by clinical medicine – that useless knowledge is, for all practical purposes, no knowledge. How to make (genetics) knowledge usable is a fundamental premise. And that process of conversion or transformation will have to be demonstrated. Now, one might have expected that measuring the success with which it achieves its objectives would have resulted in targets and performance indicators. But it has drawn back from these.

Avoidance

The CGKP has produced its first detailed work plan for 2003–4, with clear objectives, detailed aims and numerous items under each aim, but breathes hardly a word of indicators or benchmarks. Its 'deliverables', a series of reports, reviews, position papers, briefing papers, courses, alongside specific appointments, project plans and so forth, are deliberately open-ended as to both form and content.[19] 'Our view is that it is neither possible, nor advisable, to specify in detail the exact deliverables that will be achieved ... [For experience has shown] that greatest flexibility and efficiency result when detailed objectives and deliverables are agreed from year to year in response to the priorities and pressures of the time' (Zimmern 2001: 4.33). This is spelled out: when it comes to evaluating itself, 'its success will depend on achieving between all the different partners a shared vision and a degree of trust that will allow the individual objectives of each of the partners to be achieved as well a those of the Knowledge Park' (Zimmern 2001: 4.36).

The Park is *avoiding a path* it does not even have to start down. It might be an exaggeration to say this is a prophylactic or pre-emptive act (designed to avoid the problems at the end of it). But I characterise this as a (possible) drawing back because there are other signs that those who have gone down a similar path may be wanting to turn aside. A tiny movement in this direction is to be found in the programmatic statement put out by the DTI's *Quinquennial Review* of publicly funded Research Councils in the UK in 2001.[20] It traverses ground that initially sounds familiar.

At the outset, it takes multidisciplinarity as a sine qua non of the modern university. But society cannot be taken for granted. A major preoccupation is to identify a set of strategic steps in response to the need for a 'clearer strategic framework for delivering science', to "join up" with stake holders so as to work with them in a more collegiate fashion', and 'to apply principles of public service delivery ... [in] dealings with users' (DTI 2001b: 1–2). The programme sounds familiar: 'the public' emerges as a principal stakeholder. One of the public's interests is in knowing how its taxes are spent, but the need for public accountability does not stop with that rationale. Research Councils have a role in helping to promote an awareness and an understanding of science and new technologies as part of the fabric of society (DTI, 2001b: 61), in order to facilitate the involvement of the public in 'decision-making'. The explicit admonition to adopt a 'science and society' agenda, entailing consultation, engagement and dialogue, comes with the caveat that this must not be a passive matter of dissemination: the views of the concerned public should be actively sought, so that 'engagement' with stakeholders at strategic levels is of key importance: 'the aim should be to get mutual understanding, support, participation' (DTI, 2001b: 53). This must be visible and evident. 'The views of the concerned public should be actively sought ... and then subjected to the normal process of analysis. Seeking the views of the public in this way will assist better decision-making.' (What such normal processes might be is left unclear, subject to disciplinary scrutiny perhaps.)

Word for word, this could almost describe the aspirations of the CGKP. But then comes the chapter on Monitoring: 'The OST [Office of Science and Technology] and the Research Councils should devise a new performance measurement system that integrates output and performance indicators [OPIs] and benchmarking and facilitates the development of a set of critical management performance tools' (DTI 2001b: 72). Yet when one looks closely, one realises that this is not a recommendation for a totally new regime; it is an attempt to reduce and rationalise the auditing mechanisms already in place. The review specifically suggests that the number of existing measures on the Councils' performance should be smaller, that the scorecard should not be biased towards quantitative measures, that the output and performance indicators (OPIs) should be of appropriate detail, and that care should be taken not to focus on short term measures simply because they are easy to quantify – some indicators might have to be long term.

So what is the retreat from? I want to suggest that this is a retreat from a virtualism of a kind, specifically of the kind that Miller (2003) analyses, the successive displacement of the beneficiaries of policy by abstracted models that come to stand in their stead.

Dystopia

The virtualism is still there. Despite trimming the excesses, the Research Councils' programme for knowledge management is all about performance: a new *performance* measurement system that integrates output and *performance* indicators [OPIs] and benchmarking, and facilitates the development of a set of critical management *performance* tools. Performance implies exactly the production of pre-determined forms of output, and evaluation demands displays of form. Thus, in public service delivery, Miller argues, an apparent commitment to consumers and taxpayers (as the population at large) becomes encompassed by institutions of accountability (such as 'Best Value' inspection) that aggregate moral authority to themselves. They do not just aggregate moral authority, they also aggregate to themselves the authority of offering narratives of the 'real world'. The job of BV inspection, for instance, is to ensure that the service is creating improvements that would be acknowledged by the users of that service (Miller 2003).[21] This is at the heart of what Stronach, Halsall and Hustler (2002) have identified as 'evaluation in dystopian times'.

Their concerns lie with the evolution of educational policy. For forty years, they point out, evaluation rhetoric has been utopian, claiming a realist approach to the world that will deliver more consultation, less devious government and more democracy.[22] Themselves apprehending a world darkening into the 'soft totalitarianism' of education reduced to productivity, policy to performance, audit to a 'paper storm of presentational surfaces', their principal excoriations are reserved for 'evaluation'.[23] Evaluation claims to be realistic, and its touchstone is accountability; they uncover its fantastic, as in fantasy, dimensions.[24] Take, for example, global narratives of educational performance, as in the OECD league tables, the idea that educational achievements 'can be ranked, ordered into tables, and related "rationally" to the economic performance of [capitalist economies]'. A second idea chases the first: because no one believes in a direct connection, achievement and prosperity pale beside the imaging and 'symbolic function' of such rankings. Global competition, Stronach (1999) argues, is *performed* as a crisis of educational productivity, where deficiencies are tabulated, and made publicly visible and remediable through global examination. Global capitalism is re-expressed, Stronach, Halsall and Hustler say, as a *spectacle* of educational competition. When evaluate means to normatively order and symbolically perform, this is the virtual displacement of educational aims by a model of global productivity. One could go on.[25]

What is fascinating in their account is the way the tragic figure of the evaluator (the realist caught up in the virtual practices of performance) yields an 'anti-model' that turns the dystopic into a resource. The resource, if I have understood, is the kind of self-knowledge that comes from making a report *knowing* that reporting 'is never a collation of methodologically justified findings without also being a tremendous admixture of other influences'. Calculation and prediction never work out. The conflicted nature of evaluators' professional selves bears a resemblance in fact to that of other professionals, and they mention teachers and nurses. The point is simple: that conflicted subject is one which the dystopic conditions of accountability regimes have themselves created. The realisation of the impossibility of the programmatic ideal, with its promise of measurement, its indicators and targets, is a realisation of its absurdity. And that means that other apprehensions of social reality are being created at the same time. Evaluation (as I understand their message) might after all draw back from utopia, could aim to report on what is, not on what could be, and above all need not have as its aims perfection and improvement.[26] Or, to put it succinctly, in their words, why not 'anthropologise our evaluative practices'?

Such arguments about the creativity of the repressed always leave one thinking the case has already been made for repression. But then one has to count the costs. It might be better to block off some roads altogether – not to create an alternative utopia, but to anticipate and avoid some of the excesses of dystopia.

Back from the Brink

I conclude with an observation of an odd (even uncanny) fact: people do not talk much about making interdisciplinary practices accountable. I have not come across *measures* of interdisciplinary success.[27] So why have I brought these topics together? The answer will, I hope, bring us back to the question of why interdisciplinary effort must – as a cultural imperative, that is – indeed be made visible. It is in two parts.

From indicators to indexes

I pointed to the link between notions about crossing disciplines and crossing the academic–public (science and society) divide. A crucial element of the dystopia of hype, of which Stronach, Halsall and Hustler remind us, is its virtualism, the displacement of persons by their representatives (of consumers by consumer-consultants is one of Miller's examples), of practice by performance. Of course there is nothing untoward about making abstractions as such – we do it all the time. But we do not always cloak the abstractions in the language of realism. The indigenous realist claim is that they are indices, not symbols.[28] So the issue is what apprehensions of 'reality' are being conveyed. I want to suggest that the kind of material I have been discussing points to an intriguing nexus of displacements.

First, in this nexus, consider accountability as an index of society. In society and science programmes, for example, evidence that society has been taken into account is given by practices of accountability. Society may be immediately represented by funders or by consumer-consultants, but that is beside the point. To be able to point to such practices is to point to the fact that an account is being rendered 'to society'. The second question is what indexes accountability?[29] An answer I am drawn to is that interdisciplinarity can become an index of accountability. *It works as a rhetorical object for disciplinary success.* That is, insofar as interdisciplinarity carries with it the virtues conferred by communication (it would be nothing if it did not travel across disciplines) – and thus by transparency, dissemination – it is an implicit evaluation of the success *of disciplines* to convey their messages.

This conjecture of mine may not hold water for very long. But it is prompted by that uncanny fact. Perhaps one reason why people do not talk much about making interdisciplinary objects accountable is precisely this – interdisciplinarity is itself an index of accountability: an evaluator rather than the subject of evaluation. I do not mean in any formal sense, but simply that it often serves in this capacity in people's thinking about projects.

There is an extremely interesting secondary observation to be derived from this that applies directly to the CGKP. The one thing missing from CGKP's account of itself is how to measure the degree of hybridity. At its core, you will recall (see p. 74 above), is knowledge as a hybrid object: information is to be transformed 'from scientific studies on genetics into knowledge through its validation by critical appraisal, by seeking a patient and public perspective, and by placing it in its ethical, legal and social context'. On the one hand, this illustrates my point. The process of validation *is* the putting of information into an interdisciplinary context: that *constitutes* its critical appraisal. One would look in vain for a testing of the success of the validation process itself, for in this virtual context (the setting out of aims and objectives) the place of the test is already taken by the interdisciplinary process. On the other hand, the formula opens up some arresting issues that lie beyond it, and beyond the kinds of abstractions necessary to the planning of projects.

For there is a final index in my nexus. It is a thoroughly controversial element in debates and discussions, or rather it is most controversial in its virtual aspect: viz. problem-solving can serve as an index of interdisciplinarity.

A nexus of three virtual moments

1 Accountability as an index of society: Evidence that society has been taken into account lies in practices of accountability themselves.

2 Interdisciplinarity as an index of accountability: Interdisciplinarity works as rhetorical evidence for disciplinary success.

3 Problem-solving as an index of interdisciplinarity: Axiomatic evidence of the need for multiple perspectives and collaborative work.

The problem of 'problem-solving'

The problem of problem-solving lies almost entirely at level of abstract representations of interdisciplinarity. Here it emerges as an unexpected source of argument.

At first blush any equivocation seems silly. Problems and issues that arise in the real world would seem axiomatic evidence of the need for multiple perspectives and collaborative work (cf. Callon 1998, noted in the Introduction). As the Research Council Review noted (2001b: 62 [4.47]), the 'public are more often interested in the issues raised by science than by the knowledge or know-how itself. These issues are unlikely to map neatly onto the disciplinary areas covered by each Council ... Councils should consider whether the needs of their public stakeholders could be better met by further joint activities.'[30] The problem would seem to be the invocation of problems and issues in ways that make their axiomatic nature stand for the whole interdisciplinary enterprise. That is, when their invocation has a virtual or abstracting function, they subsume or obviate *collaboration*.

This is the only way I can make sense of the criticisms that arose in the debate over transdisciplinarity that Nowotny began. The charge could have been that of utopianism: everyone knows that the notion of 'problem-solving' is a phantasm – one creates ten problems for every one investigated. In fact, the charge is that the project of transdisciplinarity could be so much more.

Nowotny puts problem-solving at the heart of transdisciplinarity, and includes involvement with pressure groups: in finding solutions to 'complex problems' one needs more and more inputs, 'including those from various pressure groups ... brought to bear on the problem-formulation, design and completion of large-scale projects' (2003: 7). Moreover, her own pragmatic claim is, this leads to *better science*: 'the engineers now realise you get a better technical solution if you bring in these views' (see Cleal 2001 and Working Paper One on the Magic Lounge and the Infocity), 'This is quite a revolutionary interpretation of transdisciplinarity. It implies that more involvement on the part of society means not a better social solution, or a better adapted solution, but a better technical solution. Could not the same conclusion be applied right across the scientific spectrum: that better scientific solutions emerge if there is dialogue with society than if there is not?'

Her critics seem equally passionate in their views.[31]Basarab Nicolesceu (online response, 21 May 2003), for instance, protests at reducing the potential of transdisciplinarity to a single focus (it may be an aim, not *the* aim). Where is the subject in all this she asks (echoing Karen-Claire Voss, 8 May 2003), which I take as a question about the collaborative enterprise. Stakeholders, Voss in turn argues, are hardly adequate stand-ins for what could be a 'profoundly radical character' to transdisciplinarity. Dan Sperber (3 May 2003) points out that socially robust knowledge is usually authoritarian – transgressive contributions to knowledge find themselves pitted *against* the socially acceptable.

The 'problem' then is when the rhetoric of 'problem-solving' takes over. Problems and issues 'out there' might prompt inter- or transdisciplinary enterprises, and be the reason for it. Reasons for collaboration are not the same as the practice of collaboration. So I turn these comments into one of my own. To put problem-solving at the heart of such an enterprise is to virtualise – to take heart out of – another issue: *how to get people to collaborate.* I am imagining collaboration where what gives people value in one another's eyes is their distinctive (disciplinary) expertise.

I want to bring this to an end through two further observations. The one offers a view of multidisciplinarity routinised, where the virtual, abstracting aspects of joint collaboration are in the background. In many situations this is a regular occurrence.

Latimer (forthcoming) has described the way in which hospital consultants are able to exploit the availability of diverse narratives in multidisciplinary contexts. In their case it is to assert (and to get colleagues to collaborate in upholding?) their authority. Here one sees the difference between advocates of multidisciplinarity in a utopia of shared perspectives, better problem-identification and more democracy, and the demands posed by collaboration in ward rounds or case meetings. In her example, clinicians have to deal with those outside their discipline; they assert themselves in the way they align cultural materials, such as medical notes, with social practices, such as auditing. They can hold people to account even when they have no formal authority over the person concerned. Above all, what the consultant or clinician does is offer joined-up government in a world of distributed clinical process, by giving all the members of the multidisciplinary team their own place. What is effected is 'a continuous calling to account and a continuous division of responsibility'. Latimer emphasises that authority is asserted not through exclusion or silencing of others, but through the clinicians or consultants commandeering discourses and materials that belong to multiple domains.

The second case is aspirational, but avoids being virtual. It avoids being virtual by dint of avoiding (as far as it can) the path of indicators – by looking not for performance but for collaboration. The CGKP has numerous sites where it can find problems, and is oriented to problem-solving at the level of policy where its sees its deliverables lie. But when it comes to evaluation, the aim is to avoid an 'issue'-focused evaluation (that is a slice-of-activity approach, concentrating on one of its particular projects): the CGKP must be taken as a whole entity. One way to read this would be in terms of the many interests there are in keeping mechanisms for collaboration open and unspecified.[32]

NOTES

Acknowledgements: Principal thanks are owed to Ronald Zimmern for his encouragement of social critique, and willingness to engage with an anthropological perspective on the CGKP.

1 'Re-thinking interdisciplinarity', a project of the programme, 'Society of Information', CNRS/EHESS: http://www.interdisciplines.org/interdisciplinarity

2 A question asked, and answered, in terms at once similar and dissimilar, by James Leach (seminar paper to Department of Social Anthropology, Cambridge, May 2003).

3 The Cambridge Department of Physics and the Faculty of Mathematics are both offering courses in fundamental biology to undergraduates, which have recently been thrown open to students from the Faculty of Engineering (source: see n .4).

4 Max Perutz (1914–2002) was a chemist who worked in a physics laboratory on biological problems.

5 The following comes from the 2003 proposal to establish the Network. I am grateful to Dr Catherine MacPhee for her interest in an anthropologist's interest.

6 Citing Jantsch (1972).

7 And Nowotny sees the 'trans' of transdisciplinarity as resonating with the 'trans' of transgressive. The Branco-Weiss Fellowship scheme (see Acknowledgements) is aimed at giving natural scientists an opportunity to engage with social implications of scientific practice.

8 Gibbons (1999); expounded at length in Nowotny *et al.* (2001).

9 Some discussion is given in Strathern (forthcoming). Drawing on Franklin's (2001) formula, 'built-in-ethics', much of Hayden's current work at Girton College has been on the anticipation of ELSI questions, the way they get drawn into the preparation of products intended for the public.

10 Mode 2 in Nowotny *et al.*'s parlance: see Endnote.

11 Nowotny (2003: 7–8) writes: 'in order to [ful]fill the potential of transdisciplinarity, the notion of users must be extended. If knowledge is transgressive, then the whole range of reverse communications must be opened.'

12 At this point I leave the terms in which Nowotny presents her argument in order to get some distance on it.

13 By virtue of their interests in the exchange, each has something the other wants. This is a formal (structural) observation about exchange; on the face of it, it seemingly contravenes the rhetoric that the boundaries between science and society have been 'transgressed'.

14 Hence audit (Power 1997; Strathern 2000; Shore and Wright 1999).

15 'Once there is awareness of accountability [to different users], and this has to become part of how future researchers are educated, then it can become a way to broaden the horizon of those for whom you are producing knowledge' (Nowotny 2003: 3). On scientific citizens see Barry 2001.

16 And has attracted the interest of researchers in knowledge management and organisational behaviour. Knowledge management is a field in its own right. See Newell, Robertson, Scarborough and Swan 2002; and more generally, Moray, Maybury and Thuraisingham 2002, who discuss it as a discipline.

17 This is separate from the aim to 'stimulate the transition from research into clinical and commercial benefits through programmes and activities designed to promote intensive dissemination and sharing of genetics knowledge', which is oriented to clinical practice. From the CGKP website ('Genetics knowledge for the benefit of society'), http://www.cgkp.org.uk/about.html (May 2003).

18 Appointments have been made in Law, History and Philosophy of Science (Public Health Ethics), 'Social Science' (Sociology), as well as Primary Care Genetics.

19 And open-ended in encounters: 'We are a virtual organisation – we act as a catalyst bringing together individuals and organisations in and around Cambridge with an active interest in human genetics. But we don't try and force partnerships, they have to occur directly through concrete activities such as research programmes' (Zimmern, in an interview for *Cambridge University Newsletter* 2003).

20 DTI 2001a appears about the same time.

21 Miller deployed this to observe that 'the authority of the inspectorate is that they possess the authority of the consumer', displacing consumer fickleness by its own assurances; he goes on to note the service-provider also has to find people to consume its services – and register the improvement in terms translatable into the appropriate indicators.

22 Like evidence-based medicine in the NHS (Jan Savage), audience research in the BBC (Georgina Born), objectivity in science reporting (Monica Bonaccorso), all cases discussed at the Workshop, 'Languages of Accountability', to be collected and edited by Maryon McDonald (see end).

23 At the same time, the evaluator exemplifies the 'tragic' figure of dystopia, 'a particular mobilisation of a fractured and over-written matrix of contradictory influences, caught between various "economies of performance" and "ecologies of practice"', with reference to Stronach, Corbin, McNamara, Stark, Warne, 'Towards an uncertain politics of professionalism: teacher and nurse identities in flux', *Journal of Educational Policy*, 17: 1–30, 2002. The fix is between audit and accountability (economies of performance) and more vocational, solidary commitments (ecologies of practice).

24 Following recent writing on education, they identify 'the fantasy of the real' as turning on the real as transcendental, as unreal, as ideal, as hyper-real.

25 Policy hysteria with ever-shortened cycles of reform, multiple innovation and switching goalposts, scapegoating of professionals, and so forth.

26 That is, undo the pernicious link between measurement and target.

27 That is, where the success is in terms of the degree of disciplinary interpenetration, as one might take benchmarks as measurements of disciplinary attainment. I may well be exaggerating. Certainly the performance or collaborative outcome may be scrutinised. Monica Konrad (pers. comm.) points out the number of sci-art projects that are designed with a view to specific 'deliverables', outcomes as well as outputs. Moreover, there are very definite attempts to assess the 'impact' of cultural projects, including the impact of 'the arts' on society, measures of public access and so forth, which Selwood (2002) takes to task. [At one point she records as a complaint the fact that impact studies tend to show an organisation's engagement with the local community, rather than the actual impact of the arts programme (Selwood 2002: 9)!] I do not mean to imply that there have

been no critical studies of interdisciplinarity, or of engagement with publics.

28 From an indigenous perspective; the observer may read index as symbol. Indices, rather than 'indicators', refer not to the specific instrumentation of performance indicators, but to how the process of abstraction is annotated or indexed.

29 This is allied to a question that Power (1997) first posed: who audits the auditors? But of course it could never be answered directly, in those terms. Perhaps we should look not for super-auditing but for its representatives or substitutes in various fields.

30 The Economic and Social Research Council is invited to experiment with the notion of a research factory/hotel that might serve multidisciplinary needs if it can be linked to tackling specific problems (Commission on the Social Sciences 2003: 82).

31 From the website dialogue (see n. 1). There was also a protest at the fore-fronting of science in the discussion. Rainer Kamber (' Emancipating science, emancipated scientists', response to Nowotny 2003, 4 May 2003) asks about the 'new utopia' of science being promulgated here.

32 For this reason there is no central organisation of discussion groups or seminar networks.

REFERENCES

Barry, A. 2001 *Political Machines: Governing a Technological Society,* London, Athlone Press.

Callon, M. 1986 'Some elements of a sociology of translation: domestication of the scallops and the fishermen of St Brieuc Bay', in J. Law (ed.) *Power, Action and Belief: a New Sociology of Knowledge,* London: Routledge.

—— (ed.) 1998 T*he Laws of the Market,* Oxford: Blackwells/The Sociological Review.

Commission on the Social Sciences 2003 *Great Expectations: The Social Sciences in Britain,* London: Commission on the Social Sciences (Sponsored by Academy of Learned Societies for the Social Sciences).

DTI (Department of Trade and Industry) 2001a *Imagination and Understanding: Report on the Arts and Humanities in relation to Science and Technology,* London: Council for Science and Technology.

—— 2001b *Quinquennial Review of the Grant-awarding Research Councils,* London: Office of Science and Technology.

Franklin, S. 2001 'Culturing biology: Cell lines for the second millennium', *Health* 5: 335–54.

—— 2003 'Ethical biocapital: new strategies of cell culture', in S. Franklin and M. Lock (eds), *Remaking Life and Death: Towards an Anthropology of the Biosciences,* Santa Fe: School of American Research and Oxford: James Currey Ltd.

Gibbons, M., Limoges, C., Nowotny, H., Schwartzman, S., Scott, P., and Trow, M. 1994 *The New Production of Knowledge: The*

Dynamics of Science and Research in Contemporary Society, London: Sage Publications.

Gibbons, M. 1999 'Science's new social contract with society', *Nature* 402 (Supplement), C81-4.

Hayden, C. 2002 ' Towards an ethnography of the adverse effect', paper delivered at EASA conference for panel 'Genes, genomes and genetics', convenor G. Pálsson, Copenhagen.

Jantsch, E. 1972, *Technological Planning and Social Futures*, London: Cassell.

Latimer, J. [forthcoming] 'Commanding materials: (re)legitimating authority in the context of multi-disciplinary work', *Sociology*.

Miller, D. 2003 'The virtual moment', *JRAI* (ns) 9: 57–75.

Morey, D., Maybury, M. and Thuraisingham, B. (eds) 2002 *Knowledge Management: Classic and Contemporary Works*, Cambridge, Mass.: MIT Press

Munro, R. 1999 'The cultural performance of control', *Organization Studies* 20: 619–40.

Newell, S., Robertson, M., Scarborough, H. and Swan, J. 2002 *Managing Knowledge Work,* London: Palgrave.

Nowotny, H., Scott, P. and Gibbons, M. 2001 *Re-Thinking Science: Knowledge and the Public in an Age of Uncertainty*, Oxford: Polity.

Nowotny, H. 2003 'The potential of transdisciplinarity', from CNRS symposium on *Re-thinking Interdisciplinarity*: http://www.interdisciplines.org/interdisciplinaritypapers/5

Power, M. 1997 *The Audit Society: Rituals of Verification*, Oxford: Oxford University Press.

Selwood, Sara 2002 'Measuring culture', *Spiked Culture*: http://www.spiked-online.com/printable/00000006DBAF.htm

Shore, S. and Wright, S. 1999 'Audit culture and anthropology: neo-liberalism in British higher education', *JRAI* (ns) 5: 557–75.

Strathern, M. (ed.) 2000 *Audit Cultures: Anthropological Studies in Accountability, Ethics and the Academy*, London: Routledge.

———— [forthcoming] 'Robust knowledge and fragile futures', in A. Ong and S. Collier (eds), *Global Assemblages: Technology, Politics, and Ethics as Anthropological Problems*, New York: Blackwell Publishers.

Stronach, I. 1999 'Shouting theatre in a crowded fire "educational effectiveness" as cultural performance', *Evaluation* 5:173–93.

Stronach, I., Halsall, R. and Hustler, D. 2002 'Future imperfect: Evaluation in dystopian times', in K. Ryan, T. Schwandt and C.T. Greenwich (eds), *Exploring Evaluator Role and Identity*, Greenwich, CT: Information Age Publishing.

Zimmern, R. 2001 'The Cambridge Genetics Knowledge Park, A Proposal for the Department of Health and the Department of Trade and Industry', Cambridge: Public Health Genetics Unit.

From: CBA Workshop 'Languages of Accountability', convened by Maryon McDonald, Girton College, Cambridge May 2003. The full workshop collection will be published under this title.

ENDNOTE
Re-describing Society

In response to a timely plea for socially robust science, an anthropologist asks what it takes to render a description of society robust (and thus make it work as a reference point for science). Two empirical cases, concerning bioethics in the field of reproductive technology, and compensation claims for environmental pollution, show 'society' both too elaborately recognised, and not recognised enough. In the spirit of the original exercise, it concludes with a question about the science/society divide, and speculates on the nature of the move between Mode 1 to Mode 2 knowledge production/social forms.

At about the time the *New Production of Knowledge* (Gibbons *et al.* 1994)[1] was being written, an interdisciplinary team of experts was drafting the conclusions of the Canadian Royal Commission on New Reproductive Technologies (Minister of Government Services 1993).[2] The five commissioners who produced the final report were professionals in paediatrics and medical genetics, in the philosophy of religion, and in law; as well as a teacher-turned-business woman, and an anthropologist who was also spokesperson for a Roman Catholic archdiocese on family affairs. The government wanted to gather information with a view to legislation in an area that science had opened up for society. There were elements of 'Mode 2' knowledge production here. And, in the way developments in reproductive medicine – especially assisted fertility programmes – popularly evoked a relationship between science and society, the exercise presaged exactly the kind of 'Mode 2' interaction that was to become the focus of a second volume, seven years later. Thinking about events co-eval with *Re-thinking Science* (Nowotny *et al.* 2001), however, I am drawn to a second and rather different encounter with science.

My response to the stimulus of these two books is from social science: 'a style of reflexivity which links with contextualisation in a consciously detached manner' (Nowotny *et al.* 2001: 105n.3).[3] I offer two cases that, together, make visible some of the features that the authors identify in the transition from Mode 1 to Mode 2 knowledge production, and (in *Re-Thinking Science*) Mode 2 societies. At the least, they raise questions about the concept of 'society' similar to the question (2001: 18) that drove them to write a second volume. If science is increasingly elided with its social context, and that context starts (in their memorable phrase) 'speaking back', it turns from background into agent. So what is this 'society'? According to their account, science and society cease to operate as separate domains (they 'co-mingle'), while each retains enough gravitational pull to have distinct trajectories described as 'co-evolutionary'. My interest lies in the apparent necessity for these two entities to be seen in partnership.

One criticism can be despatched at once. The authors have done a superb job in giving us political as well as analytical tools. Political tools are needed in an era of policy formation increasingly driven by financial reasoning: we need to know how knowledge is being produced before the spending priorities are drawn up. It is also an era of increasing propertisation, where intellectual property has extracted itself from a corner of the law to occupy centre stage among a large range of ethical debates in science.[4] Claims to ownership of creative resources have become an intimate part of knowledge production. Racing alongside the uncertainties that new knowledge introduces, we witness appropriations whose stabilities (the bastions of property ownership) create instabilities of diverse kinds (exclusions and public protests). Neither of these situations lies in the authors' sights, although their insights apply to them. Their own political intention is, to put it too briefly, to have us appreciate the open-endedness and context-sensitive nature of contemporary science as strength, rather than as weakness. It is powerful to say that all the interventions and disseminations that enlarge the application of science in fact point to where we want it to go: towards a 'socially robust' science. But let me turn to other issues.

The New Production of Knowledge: A Hybrid Forum

This volume made such an impact on me, as it was the first time I had read anything which described the world – the world of work, for an academic – I knew. The authors seemed to have identified trends just waiting to be put into words. Thus, I had taken it for granted that multidisciplinary bodies, such as that appointed in the early 1980s which led to the UK Warnock Report (Warnock 1985),[5] were an application of disciplinary expertise.[6] *The New Production of Knowledge* suddenly made the phenomenon interesting.[7] The authors had caught a set of emergent practices, well illustrated by what was happening in the newly named field of bioethics. The 1990s saw huge growth in the influence of ethics committees. Internal review panels in medicine – interdisciplinary across types of medical expertise – became hybrid fora,[8] models for public debate that brought society into the picture: 'social, legal and ethical issues' was the formula.[9]

So, what is the society that is being imagined here? If science must be socially robust in order to survive, what makes 'socially' a legitimating epithet? That is, what do we need to know about society to make it work as a reference point for science? More generally, how do we produce knowledge of society that is scientifically robust?[10] What kind of information do we need to have about social conditions in order to produce an account of 'social' conditions (one acceptable *as* an account of social conditions)? What will qualify as an adequate description? And what are the consequences for the development of social science? In short, what will count as an adequate description of society in agentive mode, not just there in the background but already caught up (co-evolutionary fashion) with science?

This is where the CRC experiment is illuminating. It affords an empirical instance of an – albeit unwitting – attempt to answer some of these questions.[11] The commissioners set themselves the task of describing a society actively galvanised in response to problems posed by scientific knowledge. The Canadian people were to deliver their verdict on the future of scientific investigation, and this meant addressing and deriving information from Canadian society at large. Since Canadian society can be divided in innumerable ways, in gathering representations of all kinds, the CRC set up competing knowledge bases ('local knowledge') which had then to be brought together. Indeed, while it enquired into the views and values of 'the people', those views and values came from a society seen to be composed of diverse opinions about itself. Governance in an 'age of uncertainty': the CRC was premised on an uncertainty about how to deal with a heterogeneous population. This sense of heterogeneity was produced partly by the Commission itself, which during the course of its enquiry both drew on existing interest groups and created new ones. It was axiomatic that only plurally conceived views of a society would count.

The Mode 2 aspects of information gathering were evident. At the core lay a set of issues that only an interdisciplinary group of experts could tackle; but it was important that consultation extended to 'lay experts',[12] those who by virtue of their perspective on events rather than by virtue of qualification, stood for cross-sections of opinion. Such issues had arisen in the course of developments in medical technology: the focus was on how science should be applied. No one denied science its central role in reproductive medicine. Uncertainty lay in what people made of the possibilities – and moral dangers – and here one of the CRC's tasks was to disseminate correct information about the medical techniques. In-vitro fertilisation and associated techniques to alleviate infertility were being developed in a context frequently described as 'demand-led', with people allegedly 'desperate' for the possibilities being promised. The possibilities themselves were changing: new techniques and new knowledge about the fertilisation process emerged even as the Commission sat. Moreover, since fertility is a subject in which large sections of the population have an interest, people had began to acquire literacy in the science. Conversely, medical scientists found themselves having to refer to 'society', and there was a sense – in the late 1980s/early 1990s – in which regulation was also demand-led. While this may have been more vocal from clinicians and doctors faced with difficult choices about giving or withholding treatment, in Canada (as in the UK) many members of the scientific establishment welcomed the legitimacy that regulation would bring. This was probably more widespread at the application end (licensing clinics), but those in the sensitive area of embryo experimentation also looked to society for its sanction; research scientists and clinicians alike were caught up in the public debate.[13] In sum, reproductive medicine could be a 'type case' for Mode 2 science.

Without going into the details of the CRC's search for
society's opinion, I note that the object of control (science or
technology) emerged as at once a part of society and separate
from it, as one might imagine – and as the CRC Report does
often – 'the individual' as at once a part of society and separate
from it. Most invocations of the science versus society divide
arose when the society was ascribed an agentive capacity; the
latter had 'to do something' about the former. Conversely,
individual social enterprises (of which the scientific
establishment is one) could be imagined as distinct entities
'giving to' society, e.g. 'what science does for society'.

If every attempt to show how science and society are
implicated in one another also renews each as distinct objects
of attention, then our authors' analysis of transaction spaces
suggests an important motive. (It is also where they draw on
anthropology.) Following Galison (1997),[14] they point to
interactions between those with information to trade that need
entail no common interests or values: each side targets what it
wants. But if 'these transaction spaces are where the first
tenuous interactions between "society" and "science" take
place' (Nowotny *et al.* 2001: 147), society and science are
already present as rhetorical reference points: they offer a
common language of communication.[15] The epistemology can
be varied (Nowotny *et al.* 2001: 259n.3) but communication
has to take place. Perhaps, then, the antinomy itself creates
the possibility of a transaction space. The point is underlined
in its absence. I turn to a transaction where the common
language is not there, and where appeals cannot be made to a
relationship between science and society.

Re-Thinking Science: Accountability

The case is pertinent as to how to take context (as in 'the
context speaks back') into account in an asymmetric situation,
as might be found internal to and certainly is found external to
science-producing societies.[16] My own description starts in
Mode 2 style: the example involves science as technology,
technology in the social guise of a company involved in mineral
extraction, society as a population, and that population in
scientific guise as an object of knowledge (the people know
themselves as the possessors of 'a culture'). It concerns Papua
New Guinea,[17] one of the large-scale mines there, the
environmental devastation it has caused, and the sceptical

attitude towards science among certain local people, whose own accounts were received equally sceptically. This population was not only up against the mine, but also NGOs, the Government, and other segments of their own society. The company found its appeal to science rejected; the population was concerned with practices of verification ('science') and with social interaction ('society'), but did not name them as distinct spheres, and therefore did not try to co-mingle them. Verification and interaction were already co-mingled in the way in which they approached their problem.

Long after active representations had been made to the mine by people living in the vicinity,[18] a self-styled Papuan Pressure Group (PPG) presented a petition to the Mining Company (MC). Like many others, they demanded compensation. The Group claimed environmental damage to a river system they regarded as connected to the mine, but which the company claimed was too remote. The Group had access to specialist knowledge: a vast underground spirit tunnel meant that all the regions were in fact connected into one. However, they also knew that only what counted as scientific evidence would stick. They kept to that in their petition, and made no mention of their real knowledge about the connection between the mine and their local river systems.[19] Afterwards, they explained that they had to keep any reference to *kastom* (Melanesian Pidgin 'custom', here best glossed as 'culture')[20] out of the document because of the scepticism they knew it would encounter. They demanded K320 million (c. £100m.).

The mining company investigated the claims through a Government agency, and found there was no scientific case to answer. Bad feeling escalated, both sides claiming that the cause of any future trouble would lie with the other. The PPG leaders said that if no case for compensation were found, then they could not answer for the actions of their members. In the opinion of one outside observer (a social scientist),[21] both parties had neglected any consideration of the social and cultural factors that might lie behind the petition, and thus behind the emotion that threatened to become violent. As we have seen, PPG did so deliberately; even in their self-denial they were acting self-consciously with (scientific) knowledge of themselves as a people with a culture.[22] MC did so by refusing the parity of the knowledge that PPG had at their disposal; in their view, 'culture' threw up endless stories that people told to back their claims, and they said that the whole PPG submission was little more than a fabrication, including its purported 'science'. The observer then publicly stated his own concern – namely that, whatever else was at stake, the *consultation* process was based on incomplete analysis and understanding, and was leading to a confrontation that could be avoided. A more even-handed appreciation of the issues by both parties would lead to more equitable consultation. So his report mentioned the spirit tunnel along which people thought pollutants as well blessings could flow. However, this only strengthened the MC view that the petition rested on so many 'made-up' stories designed to exploit the company – the stories were nothing: all these people wanted was money!

The PPG petition repeats a phenomenon that recurs across Papua New Guinea.[23] Groups demand compensation for some perceived deficit, whether the resources are mineral, timber or marine, and whether for injury to their environment or in anticipation of loss of future income. Companies and sectors of the government, not to speak of the World Bank, see it all as 'too much'.

What is interesting about this case is the moment at which it occurred in the long saga of relations between the mine, the government and local people – the stage of their co-evolution. For MC had taken on some of the characteristics of a Mode 2 operation. Its policies had changed over the course of the mine's history – in part, by being forced into different kinds of relations with Papua New Guineans. Some senior MC officials talked of combining their core business with the responsibility of a 'new world' corporation, delivering development where the government could not.[24] This concealed a correlative accusation: they wanted to hold to account groups who actually lived in the vicinity for what they had done with all that had been poured into 'compensation' over the years. From the mine operators' point of view, local people wasted the money they got in royalties and other payments. The responsible (accountable) company had to act in people's interests, even when not appreciated, and it had mounted a new policy of providing sustainable development, not cash. It was not moved by fancy stories, since in its view these were just made up in order to extract as much money as possible. It could see no science in them; and as social evidence, they did little to impress.

However, the society to which this freshly self-fashioned company had to be responsive included people who had different views on the pertinence of narrative. The PPG wanted to hold the mine to account for deterioration they observed in their lands and rivers, and to make the company realise what it had done. It was precisely the stories, they held, that would achieve this. All they had to do was actually present their 'story' to the mine; description would suffice, since once the Company had seen their case, and had been put into the position of a witness, *it* would know what to do by way of remedy. Indeed, it might come up with ideas for reparation the PPG had never dreamed of! For the description would be self-evident, and have its own efficacy – making the miners 'think on' (empathise, find a place in the mind for) the plight of the victims was all they had to set in motion; it would then be up to the company how it responded.

People did not appeal to 'society'. Rather, they wanted to impress onto the miners self-knowledge of a kind – to cause them to realise the effects of their actions – and did so through giving description its own agency. While they explicitly omitted any direct reference to exotic details of culture that they thought would be a distraction, they were acting as people in possession of common self-knowledge, and they assumed that the goal of self-knowledge (that is, realisation of one's effects in the world) would apply as much to members of the company as to themselves. If I suggest that this empowerment of description was similar to the evidential force attributed to scientific explanation, then it was meant to stand *in lieu.* The opinion of one PPG leader was that even if the company's studies concerning the effect of pollutants proved negative, the company should pay out at least – say – half the compensation demanded, in recognition of the fact that local people for their part 'don't believe in science'.[25] In other words, company inability to absorb the knowledge that the PPG were presenting would be met by a refusal to countenance the company's own knowledge claims.

The kind of 'accountability' to which the Papua New Guineans subscribed does not require agreement about what each side wants from the transaction; each may have its own agenda.[26] But the PPG did wish to make that lack of agreement explicit. And if they were forced to accept the CM story, then it should be acknowledged that they were going along with it for the sake of a settlement, not because they had been convinced. 'Social robustness is a relational, not a relativistic, idea' (Nowotny *et al.* 2001: 167). While PPG were prepared to continue in relations with the company, there had to be material recognition of the relationship (that the latter had affected the former), and recognition of why PPG should be making claims at all. Hence, they envisaged monetary recompense for their forbearance. In short, they were ready to enter into a social arrangement on the basis of difference, not consensus. This created a transaction space in which scientists, but not science, could operate.

On the PPG side, then, procedures of verification were built into the interaction,[27] with an outcome we can gloss equally as 'knowledge' or 'sociality'. There was no science to be separated from society. From this perspective, the two Modes of Euro-American knowledge production come to resemble each other.

Reflection

This returns us to the question raised by *Re-Thinking Science*. Why in science-producing societies is there held to be a divide – and thus partnership – between science and society? We have seen that, where it is acknowledged, it affords a rhetorical framework for transactions.[28] But the authors intend us to see more than rhetoric in these terms. They wish, literally, to describe the kind of society that moves from Mode 1 to Mode 2 in its promotion of science.

When the 1994 volume included a chapter on the humanities, the clarity of direction fell away, for there was a strong sense in which the humanities already seemed to be operating in Mode 2.[29] Indeed, it would make nonsense in the present age to imagine the humanities in contrast with society. 'Science', however, allows the authors to express – and with considerable force, illustrate – the movement they have in mind. The antinomy, which they argue is increasingly undermined, endures as just that: it is re-invented in every realisation that the two are implicated in each other. It is this process of differentiation on which I wish to close – perhaps not the most significant extrapolation from the scope and ambition of these works, but one which points to their enormous suggestiveness.[30]

Let us take the Mode 2 state as one of self-consciousness about differentiation, for this gives it its heady sense of openness and connection. In the context of the Euro-American rise of science, such self-consciousness is brought on by new practices of scientific description, including those that make society know itself as 'society'. (A twentieth century version belongs precisely to those people who know themselves as having a 'culture'.) Mode 2 sets itself off from a pre-existing state (Mode 1), and is thus aware of the difference between the two. But it is a particular kind of society that Mode 2 envisages, one that knows itself to be open to a kind of (in our authors' epithet) distributed heterogeneity. All the ingredients for distinct pluralisms are there, but what makes for distinctiveness does not stay in one place. Expertises, local knowledges, specific voices – the reasons for uniqueness – leave their moorings.[31] Mode 1, by contrast, does not mobilise this kind of 'society'; rather, it sees various apportionments of activity, in which domains of action are taken for granted, naturalised. What lies beyond any particular domain is part of a background or context in a quiescent state. Importantly, the Mode 1 state includes not being aware of – not needing to mobilise – the difference between Mode 1 and Mode 2.

I wonder if this is not the condition of the humanities. If so, it is as much an advanced as a primitive or 'traditional' condition. If the humanities are in a state where there is no difference between Mode 1 and Mode 2, I speculate that its knowledge practices appear in a 'Mode 1' form *from having been through* various Mode 2 revolutions. The authors deal with the nineteenth and twentieth centuries but, as they hint (Nowotny *et al.* 2001: 242–3), it is characteristic of the traditional humanities to embody revolutionary precursors such as the Renaissance or (one may add) the Enlightenment – that is, radical diversifications of intellectual authority in relation to what had gone before – which subsequently produce their own antinomies. Each prior state, Mode 1, must in some sense be the resolution of a former upheaval, 'Mode 2'. This would suggest attending to how Mode 2 society re-forms as Mode 1.

The authors brilliantly place one mechanism before us. The mechanism is the way in which Mode 2 society encompasses an internal element as though it were external to itself (scientific knowledge), with the consequence that a type of society (Mode 2 society) and a type of knowledge (Mode 2 knowledge) *appear to be consonant with one another.*[32] There are two consequences of this thinking. First, when science and society seemingly reflect one another, their differentiation must be constantly re-created in order to produce the effect of convergence. Second, when both convergence and consonance become unremarkable, we enter a new Mode 1 state. Perhaps we might start looking for the precursor of this epoch, which will see scientifically robust descriptions of society, and a socially robust science: a Mode 1 state of being that has not yet begun to face up to the new challenges of whatever will then appear as Mode 2.

The CRC case gives us a good example of a Mode 2 situation sustaining both a sense of heterogeneity and a sense of making connections in all directions, with its mandate about governance driving it towards a Mode 1 consensus about scientific knowledge ('evidence based' knowledge is a cue). The PPG/MC case, on the other hand, opens up a transaction space in which a debate about knowledge is displaced by a debate about accountability. Accountability is, of course, at the heart of the argument about socially robust science, and its converse, scientifically robust accountability – the need to be well informed in order to act responsibly – is no doubt equally desirable. Yet the PPG's rejection of 'science' does not prevent them from asking how we might assess accountability.[33] We may note just how they embed accountability in relationships. This is true whether the relationships are conceptual (to do with knowledge) or personal (to do with sociality). If my rendering of the movement from Mode 1 to Mode 2 to Mode 1 seems foreign,[34] it may well be because of its (and my) relation to analogies from from Papua New Guinea(ns). For a social scientist, the 'science' that goes into scientifically robust descriptions of society is derived from many transactions; being accountable to one's (intellectual, human) sources of knowledge takes more than acknowledgment. It takes contextualisation of the kind with which Nowotny, Scott and Gibbons invite us to engage.

These are enormously stimulating volumes. The sequel to the first is also provocative: in the idea not just of 'Mode 2 knowledge production' but of a 'Mode 2 society', it unlocks a fascinating question about how one describes the sociality in question. I have tried to act the social scientist, by also turning to concrete situations in which the question has mattered.

NOTES

Acknowledgements: with gratitude for Helga Nowotny's wisdom and Roy McLeod's encouragement.

1 To repeat points made earlier (pp. 8–9, this volume), this laid out a model for changing expectations in the organisation of knowledge, especially in science, where funding is an issue. The base-line was the traditional orientation of modern, industrialised, western society, which supported research. 'In traditional society science was "external" ... and scientists saw their task as the benign reconstitution of society according to "modern' principles [Mode 1] ....In contemporary society, in contrast, science is "internal"; as a result science and research are no longer terminal or authoritative projects ... but instead, by creating new knowledge, they add fresh elements of uncertainty and instability [Mode 2]' (Nowotny *et al.* 2001: 2). Uncertainty is not a passive state: as a precondition for innovation, it is animated among other things by society's internalisation of science. The science that was once robust through its own validation procedures (Mode1) must now acquire an(other) efficacy from beyond itself (Mode 2). Insofar as society can confer acceptability, scientific knowledge makes itself robust in being seen to be 'socially robust' (Gibbons 1999). Now while Nowotny *et al.* (2001: 240) relegate need for the 'public understanding of science' to traditional (Mode 1) aims, their following comment is germane to the Mode 2 model: the realisation that more information does not necessarily lead to more empathy – rather, education encourages critical questioning, for example on the traditional distinction between experts and lay people. In this context, the formula 'Science and Society' burgeons as a rubric for research-funding programmes, and as the title a House of Lords enquiry into public perceptions of science gave to their report (Franklin, 2001: 339–40).

2 Canadian Royal Commission is hereafter CRC. I have discussed this report in two other contexts: see Strathern (1999: ch.4) and (2002: 250–67).

3 Contextualisation, briefly described below, is context given a voice ('science has always "spoken" to society ... society now "speaks back" to science [Nowotny *et al.* 2001: 50]).

4 This applies most notably in relation to patenting and the human genome. Intellectual property emerged into the limelight at the same time as audit left its moorings in accounting to assure the general public that accountability is measurable, and ethical committees have left their moorings in the hospital surveillance of specific cases to become exemplars of public scrutiny of general issues. This opening up of specialisms (specialisms in knowledge control) to heterogeneous interventions typifies the social space which the authors call the *agora* (2001: 13, 201ff.).

5 For account of the subsequent debates, see Mulkay 1997.

6 I was, though, wary of the fact that each expert then becomes a representative of his or her discipline so that such bodies lack the critical apparatus that disciplinary frameworks provide; politics or expediency or 'relevance' substitute their own measures of the expertise on offer.

7 Which begs, of course, a question about prior disposition. Here Rabinow's work has been seminal; a summary of some of his thinking on ethics in science (and the genealogy he traces to Foucault) is to be found in Rabinow (1997). This includes an exemplary enactment of the phenomenon: 'During my ethnographic works at Roche Molecular Systems I explained that as a citizen I was concerned and interested in ethical and political implications of the Human genome initiative; as an anthropologist I was attempting to evaluate claims coming from genetically oriented physical anthropologists about human behaviour; as a professor I thought I ought to know more

about how the lines between the academy and industry had changed the practice of science' (1997: 18). Among the locales in which aspects of the phenomenon have subsequently been described, see Callon 1998; Barnett 2000.

8 Nowotny *et al.* 2001: 144n.3.

9 'Social' here is partnered with elements (the law and ethical frameworks) that are simultaneously among its component domains, just as technology and science are. Note that the presence of social objectives does not in itself point to the 'strongly contextualised' procedures of the Mode 2 type; the research programme itself has to respond to 'signals from society' (Nowotny *et al.* 2001: 131). On the proliferation of ethical protocols in science see *eidem*: 202-3, illustrated by the UK Human Genetics Advisory Commission.

10 That is, one that will stand up to disciplinary scrutiny, according to the canons of social science, and more generally according to the ground rules of evidence and verification and thus produce 'objectivity' as a dimension of objectification (Nowotny *et al.* 2001: 169).

11 I refer to their efforts as experimental, because the Commission did much of the galvanising (and in some cases spread the knowledge in the first place). An immediate effect of the report was a voluntary moratorium on research in reproductive technologies.

12 See Nowotny *et al.* (2001: 227) on lay expertise and 'citizen science'.

13 Some clinicians, for example, had qualms about dealing with certain kinds of requests (e.g. when the age of the mother or the proximity of the donors seemed problematic). In the UK there were qualms over embryo experimentation, and the boundaries that defined the subject entity (the 'pre-embryo', embryo, fetus), which most notably drew science directly into the ethical debate (Mulkay 1997: n.7). The need for legitimacy was also, of course, fuelled by the prospect of being prevented in law from undertaking further work.

14 Galison's work, and the authors' extension of 'funding zones' to 'transaction spaces', are discussed by Nowotny *et al.* (2001: n.3, 214–47). Transaction spaces play a key role in their argument, in that they are 'characteristic of Mode-2 society's interaction with Mode-2 knowledge production' (*eidem*: 147).

15 That is, disparate parties who may have no other interests in common can come together through the joint rhetoric of Science and Society. For instance: how technology (Science) races ahead while ethics (Society) lags behind, or the need to support research and design (Science) which does so much for the standard of health/standard of living (Society). The CRC Report explicitly asks how the new reproductive technologies [Science] will 'change our understanding of how we relate to each other as members of society [Society]' (Minister of Government Services 1993: 45n. 2).

16 As in the 'developing countries' referred to in Gibbons *et al.*(1994: n.1, 65-66, 132).

17 The account is taken from Tony Crook's unpublished briefing paper and fieldnotes compiled in the course of a 'Property, Transactions and Creations' (PTC) study. PTC is the title of a three year ESRC-funded research project and the ESRC's support is gratefully acknowledged. I have changed the names. My particular thanks go to Tony Crook for his papers, comments and permission. See Crook forthcoming.

18 Stuart Kirsch has worked in this area for many years, and knows in detail just what such negotiations have entailed. See, for example, his chapters in the following: Miller 1993; Toft 1997; Rumsey and Weiner 2004.

19 The petition took the form of a scientific report, with numbered sections and sub-sections, and discussed issues such as sedimentation, over-bank flooding, the release of sulphur to produce acid rain, and so forth (Crook, pers. comm., 2001).

20 Sometimes called traditional knowledge, but not to be confused with the usage of that phrase in *Re-Thinking Science*.

21 Tony Crook, see note 19.

22 Scientific insofar as this way of knowing themselves brought them into the orbit of Euro-American practices of conceptualisation that have established culture as a fact.

23 Hirsch reports that, by 1999, some 156 Mining Exploration Licenses had been awarded, or were awaiting issue from the PNG Department of Mining and Petroleum, covering an area equivalent to a fifth of the whole country (Hirsch 2001: 298–312.) On compensation, see the references to claims cited in this article.

24 Their eventual response to PPG was to suggest two impact studies in response to specific complaints, concerning marine resources and the loss of migratory fish revenue. That is, they were taking their 'responsibilities' as far as they thought reasonable.

25 The petitioners were speaking for the local population, who would not have understood the science they put in the petition, either.

26 Compare Nowotny *et al.* (2001: 146n.3).

27 That is, the demonstration that suffering had its own truth. The PPG story was meant to show how they had been victims of the mine's activities. The petition also gave a list of names of others who had raised questions about the mine, to show that its effects had already been registered several times over (Crook, pers. comm., 2001).

28 The framework of 'science and society' is paralleled by analogous frameworks such as 'individual and society', and, most crucially in the CRC case, such as government (experts) and people (non-experts).

29 The authors make the general claim that the two modes co-exist, and that Mode 2 does not necessarily replace Mode 1 (Gibbons *et al.* 2001: 148n.1, 154); yet the emergence of Mode 2 is consistently placed after that of Mode 1. The second book, in accounting for social change, gives further weight to the idea of a movement in this direction (Nowotny *et al.* 2001: 15n.3).

30 In a way that barely does justice to the original impetus, but does draw from my own disciplinary knowledge.

31 Sometimes referred to as the 'homogeneity' of globalisation, a formula that no one finds satisfactory.

32 I take 'society' as the encompassing term, but it could equally well be 'knowledge' that occupies this place. Academic science (Mode 1) excludes externalities, keeping itself pure (Nowotny *et al.* 2001: 167).

33 Note the significance that our authors accord auditing (e.g. Nowotny *et al.* 2001: 235, 239).

34 '[T]he social sciences attempt to keep some kind of distancing from what they observe and interpret' (Gibbons *et al.* 1994: 92n.1).

REFERENCES

Barnett, R. 2000 *Realizing the University in an Age of Supercomplexity*, Buckingham: SRHE [Society for Research into Higher Education] and Open University Press.

Callon, M. 1998 'An essay on framing and overflowing: economic externalities revisited by sociology', in M. Callon (ed.), *The Laws of the Markets*, Oxford: Blackwell Publishers/The Sociological Review.

Crook, T. (forthcoming) 'Transactions in perpetual motion', in E. Hirsch and M. Strathern (eds) *Transactions and Creations: Property Debates and the Stimulus of Melanesia*, Oxford: Berghahn.

Franklin, S. 2001 'Culturing biology: Cell lines for the second millennium', *Health* 5: 335–54.

Galison, P. 1997 *Image and Logic: A Material Culture of Microphysics*, Chicago: University of Chicago Press.

Gibbons, M., Limoges, C., Nowotny, H., Schwartzman, S., Scott, P., and Trow, M. 1994 *The New Production of Knowledge: The Dynamics of Science and Research in Contemporary Society*, London: Sage Publications.

Gibbons, M. 1999 'Science's new social contract with society', *Nature* 402 (Supplement), C81-4.

Hirsch, E. 2001 'New Boundaries of Influence in Highland Papua: "Culture", Mining and Ritual Conversions', *Oceania* 71: 298–312.

Miller, M. (ed.) 1993 *State of the Peoples: A Global Right Report on Societies in Danger*, Boston: Beacon Press.

Minister of Government Services 1993 *Proceed with Care: Final Report of the Royal Commission on New Reproductive Technologies*, Ottawa: Government Printer (2 volumes).

Mulkay, M. 1997 *The Embryo Research Debate: Science and the Politics of Reproduction*, Cambridge: Cambridge University Press.

Nowotny, H., Scott, P. and Gibbons, M. 2001 *Re-Thinking Science: Knowledge and the Public in an Age of Uncertainty*, Oxford: Polity.

Rabinow, P. 1997 'Science as a Practice', in *Essays on the Anthropology of Reason*, Princeton: Princeton University Press.

Rumsey, A, and Weiner, J. (eds) 2004 *Mining and Indigenous Life-Worlds in Australia and Papua New Guinea*, Wantage: Sean Kingston Publishing.

Strathern, M. 1999 *Property, Substance and Effect: Anthropological Essays on Persons and Things*, London: Athlone Press.

Strathern, M. 2002 'Externalities in Comparative Guise', *Economy and Society* 31: 250–67.

Toft, S. 1997 (ed.) *Compensation for Resource Development in Papua New Guinea*, Port Moresby and Canberra: Law Reform Commisson and National Centre for Development Studies.

Warnock, M. 1985 *A Question of Life: The Warnock Report on Human Fertilisation and Embryology*, Oxford: Basil Blackwell.

From: *Minerva's* request to respond to the two volumes (*The New Production of Knowledge* and *Rethinking Science*) noted at outset. 'Redescribing society', first appeared in H. Nowotny, P. Scott and M. Gibbons (eds) 2003, 'Mode 2 revisited: The new production of knowledge', *Minerva, A Review of Science, Learning and Policy* (spec. issue) 41: 23–76. Permission to reproduce is gratfeully acknowledged to Kluwer.

OUT APRIL 2004

Mining and Indigenous Lifeworlds in Papua New Guinea and Australia

Edited by Alan Rumsey and James Weiner

This volume gives a vital and unique insight into the effects of mining and other forms of resource extraction upon the indigenous peoples of Australia and Papua New Guinea. Based on extensive fieldwork with the people concerned, it offers a comparative focus on indigenous cosmologies and their articulation or disjunction with the forces of 'development'.

A central dimension of contrast is that Australian as a 'settled' continent has had wholesale dispossession of Aboriginal land, while in Papua New Guinea more than 95% of the land surface remains unalienated from customary ownership. Less obviously, there are also important similarities owing to:

+ a shared form of land title (largely unheard of outside Australia and Papua New Guinea) in which the state retains ownership of underground resources;

the manner in which Western law has been used in both countries to define and codify customary land tenure;

+ an emphasis on the reproductive imagery of minerals, petroleum and extraction processes employed by Aborigines and Papua New Guineans;

+ and some surprising parallels in the ways that social identities on either side of the Arafura Sea have traditionally been grounded in landscape.

These studies are essential reading for all scholars involved in assessing the effects of resource extraction in Third World and Fourth World settings. Their distinctive contribution lies in their penetrating study of the forms of indigenous sociocultural response to multinational companies and Western forms of governance and law.

ADVANCE PRAISE

'*The writing is new and interesting. The essays mark out new ideas in seemingly effortless abundance... In sum – buy it, read it, I think you'll agree that its one of the really interesting books of the year.*'(**Deborah Rose**, Senior Fellow, Centre for Resource and Environmental Studies, ANU)

Alan Rumsey is a Senior Fellow in the Department of Anthropology, and **James Weiner** a Visiting Fellow in the Resource Management in Asia-Pacific Project, both in the Research School of Pacific and Asian Studies, Australian National University.
Paperback: ISBN 0-9545572-3-9 £19.50 / $35.00; Pub. Date: April 2004

order online at

WWW.SEANKINGSTON.CO.UK

Printed in the United Kingdom
by Lightning Source UK Ltd.
99086UKS00001B/35-102